# The Music Library

First published in 2005 by FUEL Publishing.

Murray & Sorrell FUEL ©
33 Fournier Street
London E1 6QE

Designed by Murray & Sorrell FUEL
www.fuel-design.com

Scans by Happy Retouching
Printed in Hong Kong

Distributed by Thames & Hudson and D.A.P.
ISBN 0-9550061-1-2

# The Music Library

Graphic Art and Sound

Conceived and compiled by Jonny Trunk

FUEL

Source music. Mood music. Library music. A forgotten but hugely important part of our vinyl history.

Its use and purpose is simple: it's well produced economic music for film, TV, advertising and radio. Never commercially available, this music was pressed from the 1950s onwards in limited quantities and then sent directly to production houses and radio stations for use when necessary.

With any new programme, producers on a budget have limited options. To commission a new theme is expensive, so it makes economic sense to use the mood music library and instantly access a wealth of well played, potentially suitable tracks. Themes from *Mastermind*, *Grange Hill*, *Screen Test*, *On The Buses*, *Budgie*, even *Terry and June* were all well placed library music cues. And its range isn't limited to TV; George Romero, the Shaw Brothers, Gerard Damiano – all cult directors – used library music to enviable effect.

From the mid-1960s onwards, as TV and radio productions increased, so did the number of library companies across Europe. All these labels bombarded potential international users with new recordings on a regular basis. This created a competitive marketplace, where a good graphic or LP title could well make a difference in the cutting room.

With restricted budgets, peculiar 'themed' music and an unusual, invisible audience, artwork for these LPs ended up in a category all of its own, as did the music. They were the soundtrack to scenes that didn't yet exist. Add to this talented session men, tight deadlines, a mass of new synthesizers, electronics and sonic fashions, and you had a unique breeding ground for very different sound.

The 1960s and 1970s were unique periods for music in the UK as the Musicians Union (MU), in an attempt to protect 'live' music and their musicians, complicated the music production system. They stated that all sessions recorded in the UK must be documented correctly, every participating musician must be credited and paid, not only for the session but whenever a track was used. This presented libraries with a beurocratic nightmare. The ruling negated the whole purpose of production music as a source of cheap and affordable sound. It led to a quiet but mass exodus across the Channel, to France, Belgium and Germany where countless sessions were safely recorded. London still had some output, but if suspicions were aroused and sessions were spotted as library, the notorious 'Dr. Death' from the MU would cancel the recordings immediately. By the late-1970s the MU finally realised the destructive influence of their ruling and lifted it.

Throughout the era some of the leading jazz, classical and avant-garde musicians across Europe and America found themselves making library recordings. Many were involved just once, others (like Alan Hawkshaw), made literally thousands of usable themes and variations for Europe and beyond. It is complicated for the library collector or archivist to trace the names of the artists, as many pseudonyms were used. Lee Mason for example, is really brassman Pete Winslow. Ipcress, a collectable Italian artist is master soundtracker Stelvio Cipriani. Artists such as Roger Roger and Nino Nardini are real names, but they both also recorded under various pseudonyms. Vocal recordings in library music are rare. Barbara Moore immediately springs to mind as one of the more successful composers and vocalists in this area. Other scat or wordless vocal artists are out there too, but few real songs are to be found anywhere. An exception are the Electric Banana LPs issued by De Wolfe in the late-1960s, whose sought after mod-like recordings feature members of the Pretty Things.

As is evident in the pages that follow, there are and have been numerous labels and manufacturers of source music. Many of these labels are still active today, while some have been swallowed up by larger conglomerates, others have disappeared without a trace. Adding to the complication and interest in collecting are the seemingly endless lost and unique labels that have resurfaced over the last few years. Robert Vigier, Nike and Bang Bang are all examples of obscure labels with no apparent history, archive or new owners. No doubt other libraries will remain lost.

As CDs started to make their ugly way into our lives, libraries stopped producing vinyl and this large, cumbersome format was rapidly replaced. Throughout the 1980s and early-1990s much of the vinyl sitting idle in TV and radio stations was destroyed, skipped or just given away. By the mid-1990s, adventurous music collectors started to listen back. New and different sounds were being found on these old neglected LPs – weird beats, odd instrumentations, albums full of dark jazzy interludes or bizarre garage rock. Word spread about these LPs, and finding and collecting them became difficult and expensive as prices for these non-commercial pressings began to escalate. Either in clubs, through the sampler or from exotic home listening, library music was enjoying a small renaissance which continues today.

This book brings together an archive of vintage library records assembled by some of the top UK collectors. This is not a buyers guide, or by any means a completists catalogue. It's a visual and audio celebration of some of the greatest unseen sleeves and unheard music ever made.

Jonny Trunk

Pop too poppy? Rock too rocky? Funk too funky? Jazz too jazzy? Classical too classical? Avant-garde too avant-garde? Don't worry, there is an alternative… a kind of fusion of all these elements – library music. So what is it about library music?

Since the 1950s two of library music's favourite themes seem to have been those features of modern life – 'activity' and 'apprehension'. (Don't worry there's deep sea diving and space exploration too). The best library albums and tracks sound like some of the most modern music ever made. They have that same 'out of this world' feel which is present in all sorts of so called 'background' music. (Similar in feel, incidentally, to the hotel lift Muzak I heard while The Specials were on tour in America in 1980, which inspired me to try and incorporate it into the band's second album – a move regarded as so radical at the time it was described as 'commercial suicide'). Library music seems to get every musical genre just slightly wrong enough to sound a bit twisted and different, (i.e. great). It created a sort of super genre all of it's own. Some of it is just pure… library, it doesn't sound quite like anything you've ever heard before. Library was intended to extract the 'mood' from all sorts of music, and sometimes it seems to capture the feel of an era better than the music which was actually sold at that time. If you want to find that strange ingredient which makes modern music modern, futuristic library music isn't a bad place to look.

Maybe library music's strange appeal has something to do with the musicians being heard and not seen. There are no pictures of them on the record sleeves, no personality cult, no fashion, no looks or age to confuse things. Another plus is that not a note of this music was ever played live, or sold directly to the public, so irrelevant irritations like audience reaction or 'commercial viability' weren't really a consideration either. This was a sort of underworld, where the record buying public or critics wouldn't dream of venturing. To create different 'atmospheres', musicians could do whatever came into their heads, and they did, without any restrictions – apart from the fact that they had an album to make before lunch of course – not much time for self indulgence.

Some of the musicians were well respected modern classical, film or accomplished jazz composers, probably in need of extra cash. The daughter of Italian composer Paulo Renosto says he found real creative freedom in the world of library music under the name of Lesiman, away from his struggles in the world of film and classical music (page 201-202). There were other great library musicians who were complete 'failures' in the 'real' music world. Their only legacy is the library music they made, either for a fee, or in the hope that someone somewhere would choose their track as a soundtrack for a TV drama, science programme, radio play, B-movie or porn film. How much of their output ever actually got used is anyone's guess. Perhaps there is a note of bitterness detectable in some of this 'outsider' music, a result of the lack of recognition the musicians received. A poor composer could have put his heart and soul into what might have been billed as a 'Modern religious mass for orchestra and arp synthesizer', only to have it chopped into short sections entitled '*Octopus Approaching*' or something similar. A library label boss might have decided to add a fairground waltz or a foxtrot, by a completely different artist, to some dark modern masterpiece. (We could be talking 'blue-cheese-flavoured-avant-garde-orchestral-with-a bit-of-fuzz-box-guitar-thrown-in' type dark modern masterpiece here).

Current interest in old library music may have been started by hip hop producers looking for a breakbeat or a loop, and post-rare groovers or acid jazzers searching for that full length funky track, but there are other noises as well. Library musicians were cutting costs by using drum machines and sequencers ever since they were invented for home organs. They can probably be counted among the pioneers of that peculiar electronic European beat music which later crossed the Atlantic and became electro and techno, so there's plenty of sick stuff from the eighties in there too. There are great library reggae tracks; for the rockists, there's everything from sixties garage to low budget prog, maybe there's even a library punk album somewhere, in some dirty storage unit, just waiting to be discovered. (This would almost have to be the ultimate punk record).

If the serious avant-gardists are getting into some of the abstract, ambient, experimental, and electronic library music now, they have been a bit slow on the uptake – not good if you're an avant-gardist. Maybe they didn't know what to make of library music at first? Was it 'Musique Concrete' or 'Musique Tetrion Fillere'? Does it matter, as long as it sounds good? Did Delia Derbyshire for example, who made some library music, (as well as 'sound effects' for the BBC and *Doctor Who*), see herself as a 'serious modern electronic composer' or not? Who cares? Her music sounds exactly the same either way. Apparently when avant-garde German electronic composer Karlheinz Stockhausen went to hear avant-jazz spaceman Sun Ra, he couldn't understand how Ra could do versions of Walt Disney songs. Ra was also supposed to be a fan of that knight of exotica, Les Baxter. Some of the more experimental library music seems like a European parallel mixture of so called 'cheesy', and 'avant-garde' elements. Library musician Gampiero Boscemi could slip quite happily from swinging Lowrey home organ melodies, to free form avant-garde 'cat walking up and down the keyboards' style (as it was known up north). Boscemi even recorded a track called *Kitty on the Moogboard.*

Many track titles in library music are great in themselves, how about: *Millstone Grit, Nightmare on LSD, Cogweb,* or *Moonlight over McAlpines* (capturing the atmosphere of a deserted building site at night)? The album title *Action Printing,* (page 171), has to be the craziest description for music ever. Library sleeves normally carried descriptions of the music on each track. Do you require: 'Heavy Sliding Sounds', 'Industrial Pop Movement' or 'Medium Rock'? Maybe, thankfully, the vast majority of library records don't have any lyrics. As a punter you will have often been ordered to 'party hearty', or 'shake that booty,' but have you ever actually been asked to 'touch... touch your eyebrow'? (*Magical Ring* page 35).

Don't ever let anyone sell you a library record until you've heard it. As any library crate digger will confirm, a large proportion of the vast amount of library music made is the most indescribable dreck, and would break the mind of even the most warped library freak. Some of the music on the records I lent for this book is amazing, but I bought a few of them dirt cheap just for one track, or sound. I even bought a couple for next to nothing, just for the sleeves.

Some libraries actually used the same artwork for all their albums and took a bit of time getting it right, with other sleeves it's hard to see a connection with anything at all, let alone the music inside – a 'roadkill' in stitched canvas? (*Andros* page 161). What has that volcano, (made from crumpled silver foil and red liquorice strings), got to do with light spacey jazz funk? (*Amazing Space* page 176). What are Chairman Mao's revolutionary workers doing with an athlete jumping over them, all neatly wrapped in a nice folder fastened with a belt (canvas, naturally)? (*Batterie* page 150). Did you notice the hideous human form trapped inside the body of the wolf? (*Red Kite* page 159). The same brief seems to have been given to the sleeve designers as the musicians – 'zero budget and complete and utter artistic freedom to indulge in your most disturbed inner fantasies'. My favourite among the covers I lent for this book, is the one where someone is being savaged by an Alsatian on a bleak mountain slope. (*Carosello Musicale* page 94). What more could you want from an album sleeve? Could it be a still from a police dog training film, meant as some sort of political comment on the Italian Fascist Party's links with the police force? I doubt it. (Although apparently Italian politicians did sometimes play library music in the background to enhance their public speeches).

A last word of warning. Once you descend to search the dark basements of library, ordinary music may never sound quite the same again. *Dark Basements* is the title of a library track itself. There is no way out. DJs Anonymous don't have a helpline either.

**Jerry Dammers**
Founder of The Specials and 2 Tone

# AMPHONIC

Standard Amphonic sleeve,
stickered with later address. (JT)

**Moodsetter Pacesetter** Amphonic 1000 Series
James Clarke
Includes *Wild Elephants*. (JT)

HISTORY: Founded in 1970 by artist and arranger Syd Dale. Based in Mortimer Street, London, eventually moving to Bromley, Kent. OUTPUT: Wide variety of bright compositions. Only eight releases on the more dramatic 1000 series. STYLE: Easy, classical, jazz, drama, catchy big band sounds. MUSICIANS OF NOTE: Syd Dale, Johnny Pearson, Tony Hatch, James Clarke. SLEEVES: Generic yellow, followed by 1000 series in blue and grey. FAMOUS CUES: *Wish You Were Here* theme.

**April Orchestra Lard Free** Volume 15
Gilbert Artman
Heavy progressive jazz rock and electronics. (SS)

**April Orchestra** Volume 3
Ennio Morricone
Sounds of suspense. (JH)

HISTORY: Large international library label affiliated with RCA and CBS. OUTPUT: Worldwide licensed recordings from important filmic composers. International releases and pressings. STYLE: High-end dramatics, experimentation, electronics, rock, classical. MUSICIANS OF NOTE: Ennio Morricone, Gabriel Yared, Michel Magne, The April Orchestra. SLEEVES: Some inconsistencies, generic fonts, random colour changes, occasional graphics.

**April Orchestra** Volume 4
A. Ricardo Lucians
Tension cues. (JH)

**April Orchestra** Volume 5
D. I. Jarrec
Electronic, avant-garde. (JH)

**April Orchestra** Volume 7
Ennio Morricone
Musical suspense. (JH)

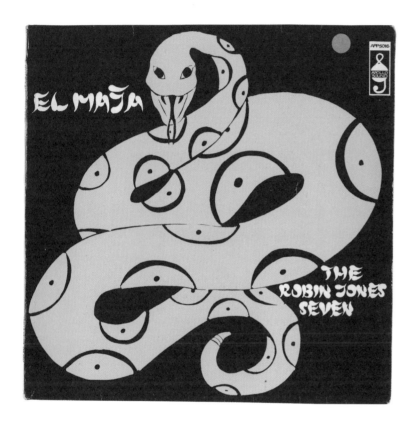

**El Maja**
The Robin Jones Seven
Latin jazz. (SS)

**Denga**
The Robin Jones Seven
More latin jazz. (JT)

HISTORY: London based library founded by Heinz Herschmann in 1964. OUTPUT: Above average-sized catalogue. International releases. Strong Polish and Swiss connections. Some LPs commercially available. STYLE: Easy listening, harder percussion, scat, latin jazz, world music, big band sounds. MUSICIANS OF NOTE: The Novi Singers, Polish Radio Orchestra, Robin Jones. SLEEVES: Various themed series. Robin Jones LPs have a unique, unmatched look. FAMOUS CUES: Numerous test card numbers, jazz dance classics.

**Melody & Rhythm** Volume 1
John Fox and David Lindup
Various easy cues. (JT)

**Colours in Rhythm** Volume 4
Ted Nord
Jazz and easy numbers. (JT)

ANDRZEJ KURYLEWICZ

CONTEMPORARY MUSIC FORMATION

AS 1016
STEREO

APOLLO SOUND

**Contemporary Music Formation**
Andrzej Kurylewicz
Jazz and avant-garde sound. (JH)

# ARIETE

## Musica per commenti sonori

CO 10005

| LATO 1 | | LATO 2 | |
|---|---|---|---|
| 1) SWEET-BEAT | 3'51" | 1) MOTUPROPRIO | 4' |
| 2) INTERRUPTED | 3'33" | 2) FREE STUFF | 2'30" |
| 3) REPETITION | 3'45" | 3) WAWA | 3'36" |
| 4) STARTER | 3'30" | 4) POLYPHONY | 2'33" |
| 5) MAKKARESH | 3'54" | 5) GRACE | 5'02" |
| 6) FAST TRAIN | 2'30" | 6) FLYER | 1'44" |

Musiche di Stefano TOROSSI
Complesso BRUGNOLINI - TOROSSI

Musiche di S. BRUGNOLINI
Complesso BRUGNOLINI - TOROSSI

**Musica per commenti sonori**
Stefano Torossi
Psychedelic jazz cues and more.
Ariete / Constanza label. (JG)

HISTORY: Established in Italy c.1968. Based in Milan. OUTPUT: Primarily a soundtrack label, moving to short runs of source music based on original soundtrack recordings. Poor distribution. Sub-licensing with Constanza Records. Distribution via Carosello. STYLE: Most LPs feature a broad musical cross section. Some vinyl pressing inconsistencies and faults. MUSICIANS OF NOTE: Franco Micalizzi, Gino Marinuzzi, Riz Ortolani, Gianni Ferrio, and Mario Nascimbene. SLEEVES: Standard simple design with colour variations. Complex international sleevenotes.

## BACKGROUND MUSIC
## PUBLISHERS (BMP)

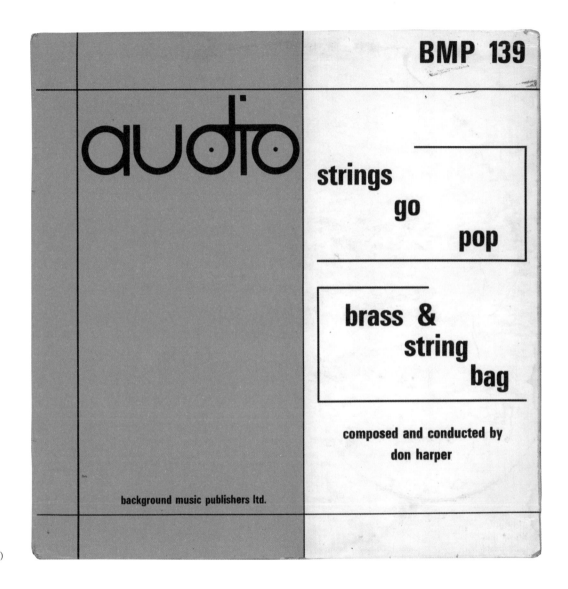

**Strings Go Pop**
Don Harper
Mystery and comedy with electric violin. (LV)

HISTORY: Short lived London based label, subsidiary of Joseph Weinberger, c.1970. OUTPUT: Small but diverse. STYLE: Classic pop backgrounds, easy listening, some electronics. MUSICIANS OF NOTE: Don Harper. SLEEVES: Generic house graphic style.

# BANG BANG

**Astrattismo 2**
Franco Delfino
Drama, sex, small orchestra and effects. (S)

HISTORY: Independent, obscure Italian label. Milan based, c.1970.  OUTPUT: Very limited releases, perhaps only twelve.  STYLE: Standard dramatics and underscores with some electronic effects.  SLEEVES: Classic one colour Op-art styles.

Various artists
*Jazz on a Summers Day* soundtrack.
Standard BBC sleeve. (MG)

HISTORY: In house library label for the BBC.   OUTPUT: Small, only for worldwide BBC TV and radio usage.   STYLE: All musical styles, some cover versions and internationally licensed tracks, even some rare soundtrack recordings pressed as library.   SLEEVES: Generic house sleeve, simple variations in colour.

**BEAT**

A New Harmonica Colour No.3
Franco De Gemini
Groovy and light atmospheres
with electric harmonica. (PW)

HISTORY: Well known Italian soundtrack label, started c.1974. OUTPUT: Very few library recordings exist, possibly only five. STYLE: Classic spaghetti style themes, with and without beats. MUSICIANS OF NOTE: Alessandro Alessandroni, Franco De Gemini. SLEEVES: Photographic.

# BERRY MUSIC

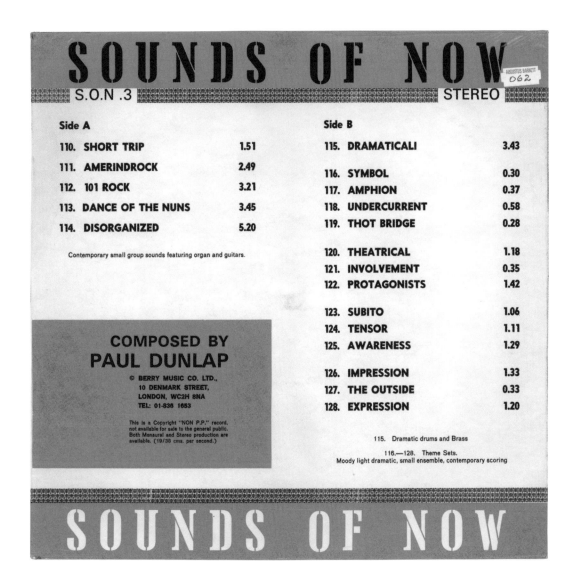

**SOUNDS OF NOW**

S.O.N .3                                                STEREO

**Side A**

| 110. | SHORT TRIP | 1.51 |
|------|-----------|------|
| 111. | AMERINDROCK | 2.49 |
| 112. | 101 ROCK | 3.21 |
| 113. | DANCE OF THE NUNS | 3.45 |
| 114. | DISORGANIZED | 5.20 |

Contemporary small group sounds featuring organ and guitars.

**COMPOSED BY**
**PAUL DUNLAP**

© BERRY MUSIC CO. LTD.,
10 DENMARK STREET,
LONDON, WC2H 8NA
TEL: 01-836 1653

This is a Copyright "NON P.P." record,
not available for sale to the general public.
Both Monaural and Stereo production are
available. (19/38 cms. per second.)

**Side B**

| 115. | DRAMATICALI | 3.43 |
|------|-----------|------|
| 116. | SYMBOL | 0.30 |
| 117. | AMPHION | 0.37 |
| 118. | UNDERCURRENT | 0.58 |
| 119. | THOT BRIDGE | 0.28 |
| 120. | THEATRICAL | 1.18 |
| 121. | INVOLVEMENT | 0.35 |
| 122. | PROTAGONISTS | 1.42 |
| 123. | SUBITO | 1.06 |
| 124. | TENSOR | 1.11 |
| 125. | AWARENESS | 1.29 |
| 126. | IMPRESSION | 1.33 |
| 127. | THE OUTSIDE | 0.33 |
| 128. | EXPRESSION | 1.20 |

115.   Dramatic drums and Brass

116.—128.   Theme Sets.
Moody light dramatic, small ensemble, contemporary scoring

**SOUNDS OF NOW**

**Sounds Of Now** No.3
Paul Dunlap
Includes *Dance Of The Nuns*. (JG)

HISTORY: Established by Roy Berry in London, late-1950s. Now owned by KPM.  OUTPUT: Large and varied. Some experimentation.  STYLE: Underscores and classic early mood themes.  MUSICIANS OF NOTE: Eric Siday, Paul Dunlap.  SLEEVES: Simple graphic and typographic styles, occasional photography.

SBH 3018

**Boosey &
Hawkes**

Background Music
Specially recorded for
Film Radio & Television

Generic Boosey & Hawkes sleeve.
Multiple drama cues. (JT)

HISTORY: Boosey & Co traceable to a music lending library in London, 1760. Merged with Hawkes in 1930. Vinyl based library started mid-1950s. OUTPUT: Vast number of international releases. STYLE: Known for classical, symphonic music, dramatics, industrials, jazz, pop and some electronics. MUSICIANS OF NOTE: Sam Fonteyn, Trevor Duncan, Jeff Bastow, John Scott. SLEEVES: Generic vortex and wave design. FAMOUS CUES: Some *Scooby Doo* incidentals.

# BOSWORTH MUSIC

BLP 102                                           33⅓ r.p.m.MONO

**BOSWORTH BACKGROUNDS**

ELECTRONIC MUSIC
Composed and performed by
VACLAV NELHYBEL

**❶**
1. Cosmic Awakening
2. Cosmic Breath
3 Cosmic Cycle
4. Cosmic Dawn
5. Cosmic Fright
6. Cosmic Twilight
7. Dark Cosmic Clouds
8. Space Meteors
9. Space Ship
10. Space Spirals
   Interplanetary Journey
11. Slow Mysterioso
12. Agitato
13. Spasms

**❷**
1. Strange Eruptions
2. Nebulae
3. Song of the Spheres
4. Star Clusters
5. Mars Craters
6. Pulse of the Universe
7. Sun Lava
8. Ionosphere
9. Vibrations in Outer
                    Space
10. Voices from Outer
                    Space
   Atmospheric Reactions
11. Slow rising cosmic
              Excitement
12. Woodwinds in Lyrical
              Interlude
13. Electronic finish with
    Woodwinds

**BOSWORTH MUSIC**

LONDON        KÖLN        WIEN

Vaclav Nelhybel
Electronic music and effects.
Early 10" release. (JT)

HISTORY: London library with satellites in Berlin, New York, Brussels and Vienna. Established through sheet music production (Leipsig 1889), in London by 1892. Moved into 78rpm production during the 1930s, then to 33rpm production in 1966. Now owned by the Musicsales Group. OUTPUT: Small international catalogue, broad in appeal. STYLE: Classical, light classical, jazz, easy listening, avant-garde. MUSICIANS OF NOTE: Johnny Teupen, Paolo Zavallone, Klaus Doldinger. SLEEVES: Generic blue sleeve on 10", slight changes in tone and typeface. Colour changed to yellow in late-1970s, then to photography. FAMOUS CUES: *This is Your Life* door sting.

MUSIC FOR TELEVISION, FILM, RADIO                    HARMONIC MUSIC LIBRARY

# THEMES
# IN
# BEAT

BRULL
CBW 660

**Themes In Beat**
H. Thieme
Various atmospheric cues. (JG)

HISTORY: London label, started in the late-1960s, affiliated to Harmonic. Also known as 'C. Brull'.  OUTPUT: Small number of original releases, but large international licensing and re-labelling of continental catalogues such as PSI.  STYLE: Standard and contemporary mood themes.  MUSICIANS OF NOTE: Gert Wilden, Hans Posegga, Trevor Duncan.  SLEEVES: Simple, plain typographic style.

# BRUTON

**Heavy Rock** BRH Contemporary Series
Various artists
Features futuristic disco. (JT)

**Electrofx** Volume 1 BRI Series
James Asher
Modern electronics. (JD)

HISTORY: London label, founded in 1977 by Robin Phillips (see KPM), as part of the ATV empire. Named after Bruton Street where it was originally formed. Briefly owned by Michael Jackson, currently owned by BMG / Zomba. OUTPUT: Wide and varied releases, prolific pressings, internationally distributed. STYLE: Broad musical palette. MUSICIANS OF NOTE: Francis Monkman, Brian Bennett, Alan Hawkshaw. SLEEVES: Early sleeves all based on the twelve cube graphic device. Albums are colour coded for genres i.e. orange for futuristic themes and green for fanfares, links, bridges. FAMOUS CUES: Incidentals for *Space 1999*, *The Sweeney* and *The Krypton Factor*.

# CAM

MUSICA PER COMMENTI SONORI TRATTA DAL FILM «LOVE BIRDS»
Musiche di BRUNO NICOLAI

SELECTIONS FOR MUSICAL SCORES FROM THE MOTION PICTURE «LOVE BIRDS»
...res of BRUNO NICOLAI

MUSIQUE POUR MOTIFS SONORES TIRÉE DU FILM «LOVE BIRDS»
Musiques de BRUNO NICOLAI

MUSIK FÜR TON-UNTERGRÜND AUS DEM FILM «LOVE BIRDS»
Musik von BRUNO NICOLAI

MÚSICA PARA COMENTARIOS SONOROS TOMADA DEL FILM «LOVE BIRDS»
Autor de la música BRUNO NICOLAI

DISCO DI SONORIZZAZIONE          DISQUE DE SONORISATION
SCORING RECORD                   BESCHALLUNGS PLATTE
DISCO DE SONORIZACIÒN            DISCO DE SONORIZAÇÃO

**Love Birds**
Bruno Nicolai
Soundtrack pressed as library cues.
Generic blue CAM sleeve. (JT)

HISTORY: Formed in 1962. Acronym for Cinema's Musical Artists. Predominantly a soundtrack label, however many original scores were repressed and repackaged for synchronisation. OUTPUT: Vast number of international releases. Numerous library series. STYLE: Broad range of small group sessions, classical scores and countless electronic recordings. MUSICIANS OF NOTE: Ennio Morricone, Giampiero Boneschi, Piero Piccioni, Bruno Nicolai. SLEEVES: Generic blue big 'C' artwork, series variations of orange, red, green and grey / green. FAMOUS CUES: *Escalation* and *Love Birds*.

**Up Up and Go Girls** Release No. 6
Produced by Ole Georg.
Vocal scat tracks. (JT)

**Bass Patterns** Release No. 7
Produced by Ole Georg.
Various jazz forms. (JD)

HISTORY: Established c.1970 as part of the giant Capitol Records label. OUTPUT: Nine series of ten releases, few original recordings, most licensed from Europe. Rare. STYLE: Jazz, rock, electronics etc. Standard library thematics. Mostly short cues. MUSICIANS OF NOTE: No artists credited. SLEEVES: Generic tower image, with simple reverse grid. Colour variations for each series.

# CAROSELLO

**Feelings**
Stefano Torrosi under a pseudonym.
Progressive easy and funky jazz.
Later issued on Conroy Eurobeat. (JG)

HISTORY: Milan based soundtrack label established mid-1960s. OUTPUT: Recordings licensed to large library labels such as Conroy. STYLE: Jazz, easy, filmic. MUSICIANS OF NOTE: Pino Donnagio, Stefano Torrosi. SLEEVES: Photographs.

# CAVENDISH

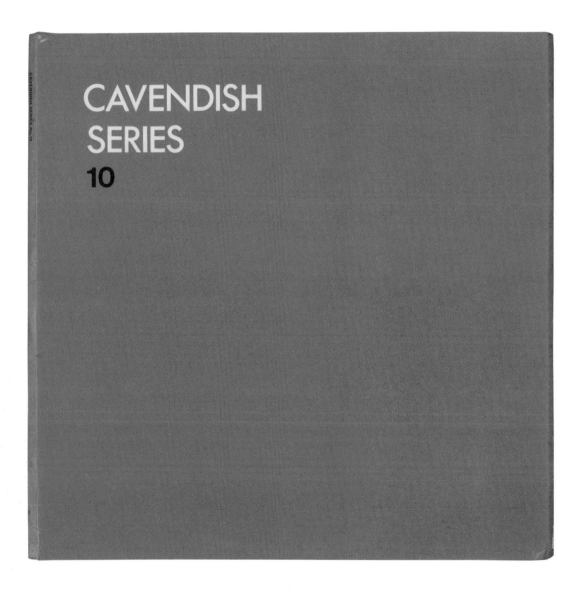

Cavendish Series 10
Various artists. Vocal recording.
Rare and unusual three sided, double LP. (JT)

HISTORY: **Based in Regent Street, London c.1973. A small subsidiary label to Boosey & Hawkes.** OUTPUT: **Small and limited.** STYLE: **Simple themes and dramatics, easy, some vocals.** MUSICIANS OF NOTE: **Harry Stoneham, Syd Dale, Ray Davies.** SLEEVES: **Generic red / pink.**

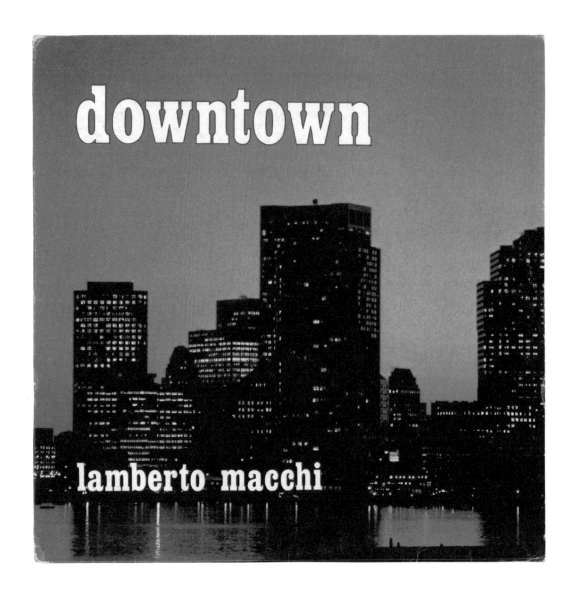

**Downtown**
Lamberto Macchi
Progressive urban sounds. (JD)

HISTORY: Paris based label, c.1975.  OUTPUT: Quite small. Limited European distribution.  STYLE: Standard dramatic sounds, some modern instrumentation.  SLEEVES: Stock photography and type.

# CENACOLA

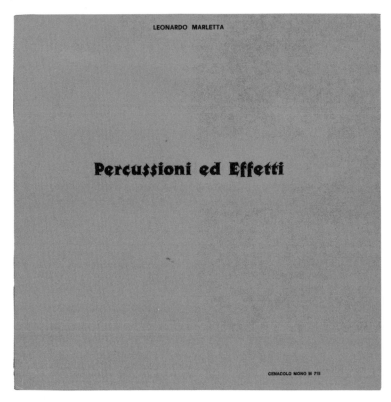

**Il Mondo Dei Giovani** Volume 4
Maqx Rocci and his friends. (I)

**Percussioni ed Effetti**
Leonardo Marletta
Treated percussion. (JD)

HISTORY: Rome based, mid to late-1970s. Started by Italian jazz legend Umberto Santucci. OUTPUT: Small to medium sized, but with poor distribution. Early issues scarce.
STYLE: Mainly jazz based recordings. SLEEVES: Early sleeves have popular art covers, later sleeves feature simple typography.

# CHARLES TALLAR

**Space Résonances**
World Trade Center sleeve.
Licensed to Music Media. (JD)

HISTORY: Small Paris based label started in 1975. OUTPUT: Very small, with some international licensing. STYLE: Contemporary mood music, themes and underscores. SLEEVES: Stock photography.

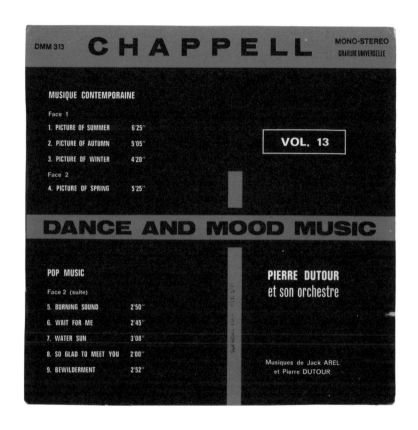

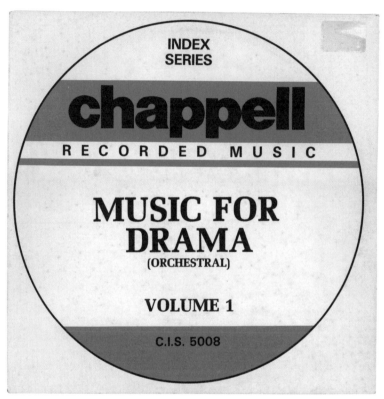

**Dance and Mood Music** Volume 13
Jack Arel and Pierre Dutour
Concept rock meets pop. (JT)

**Music For Drama** Volume 1
Various artists
CIS Compilation Series. (JT)

HISTORY: Started in 1811 with sheet music publishing in London. Source music recordings began in 1941. Overseas offices established early-1960s. OUTPUT: A vast international catalogue – possibly the largest worldwide. (See also TVMusic). STYLE: All genres catered for. MUSICIANS OF NOTE: John Barry, Ennio Morricone, Nino Nardini, Roger Roger, Johnny Hawksworth, Mark Duval, Jean-Claude Petit, Jack Arel, and more. Some pseudonyms. SLEEVES: Early yellow house sleeves, basic white and red compilation sleeves, various two-colour international sleeves with variations in tone, graphics and photography. Long LPC Series in yellow, blue and later graphic art.

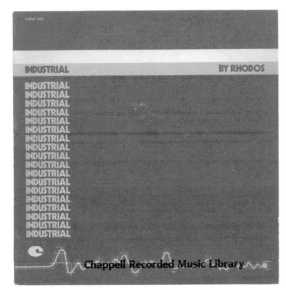

**Mood Music Volume 26** CMM Series
Rene Costy
Jazz. Rare French 'dice' sleeve. (JG)

**Industrial** CHAP Series
Rhodos
Conceptual music. Late-1970s. (JD)

**"A Ecouter"** French CHA Series
Richard Demaria
Synthesizer and percussion. (LV)

**Wild Side** Late LPC Series
John Cacavas
Urban themes by cult film composer. (SS)

**Brass and Rhythms** LPC Series
Mark Duval and his Music
Includes *The Loner*. (JT)

**Music by Lee Mason** LPC Series
Pete Moore (pseudonym)
Jazz and scat. (JT)

**Pop Sounds / Mad Dog** LPC Series
David Holland
Various pop cues. (JT)

**Electronic Music / Synthesizer Effects** LPC Series
The Allsorts / The Machines
Fine electronic and synthesizer cues. (JM)

**Themes Medicaux**
William Gum-Boot
Experimental and progressive. (JD)

**"Magical Ring"**
J. P. Decerf
Unique rock and vocal sounds. (JD)

HISTORY: Editions Musicales Chicago 2000, established in Paris c.1972. Independent. OUTPUT: Small, unpredictable, strange catalogue numbering system. Possibly distributed by Capitol Records. STYLE: Jazz, pop, experimental rock. SLEEVES: Mostly two-colour illustrations.

# COLOURSOUND

**Fly Me To The Sun**
Andre Mikola and Andrzej Marko
Contemporary group sounds - nature and industry.
Artwork by Waltraud Greffenius. (JD)

**Input Output**
Various musicians including Marek Bilinski.
Research, production and success themes.
Artwork by Waltraud Greffenius. (JD)

HISTORY: Munich based experimental, progressive library. Established c.1979. OUTPUT: Large, European distribution, with the help of Warner Music. STYLE: Modern sounds based on contemporary ideas and technology. Some licensed recordings. MUSICIANS OF NOTE: Joel Vandroogenbroek (of Brainticket), Alessandro Alessandroni, Klaus Weiss. SLEEVES: Varied and colourful artwork of differing quality. Full colour back covers.

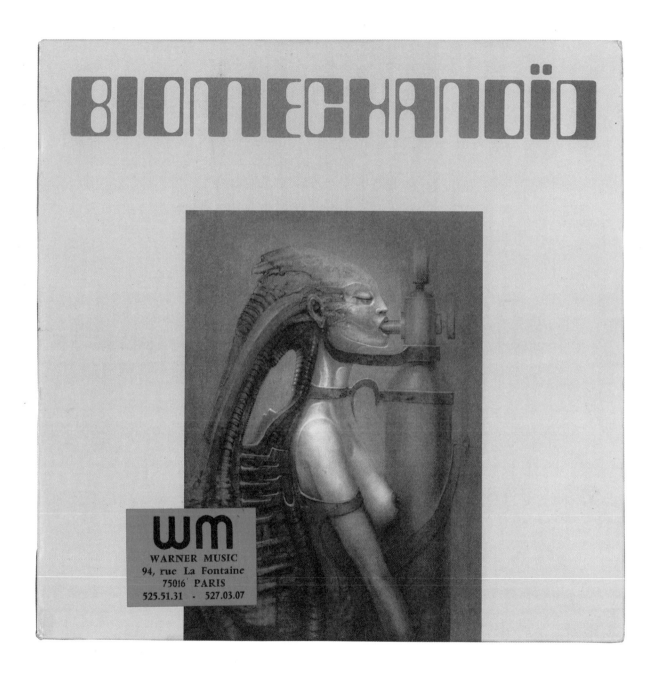

**Biomechanoïd**
Joel Vandroogenbroek
Conceptual, futuristic electronics.
Artwork by H. R. Giger. (JT)

# CONROY

EURO 4

ROMANTIC BACKGROUNDS

CONROY Eurobeat RECORDED MUSIC LIBRARY

**Romantic Backgrounds**
Conroy Eurobeat Series
A. Alessandroni wordless vocal cues. (JT)

HISTORY: Established in 1964 by music composer Dennis Berry, (aka Peter Dennis), as part of the older Berry Music Library. OUTPUT: Extensive and very varied catalogue. Some original sessions, and for the later Eurobeat Series others were licensed from Italy and Germany (from libraries such as Sermi and Carosello). STYLE: Wide ranging, some electronics, slightly exotic productions. MUSICIANS OF NOTE: Larry Robbins, Sam Sklair, Klaus Weiss, Stefano Torrosi, Bruno Nicolai, Bruno De Filippi. SLEEVES: Early Conroy sleeves have 'record design', followed by the orange CON ROY graphic sleeves. Later Berry Music Series with orange graphic sleeve. Short Eurobeat Series in blue.

**Larry Robbins Percussion / Underdrama**
S. Burdson and G. Narholz
Standard 1970 Conroy sleeve. (JT)

**London's Underground**
L. Paul-Phillips
Hard rock, said to include Dave Brock from Hawkwind, 1972. (C)

# CONTACT

**Thanks for Listening** Series 3
Fritz Maldener
Jazz and slight psychedelia. (I)

HISTORY: Small independent German label. Little traceable history. OUTPUT: Prolific. Series of albums issued across Europe, briefly distributed by Berry Music in the UK. Rare. STYLE: Jazz and mood based, easy. SLEEVES: Simple two-colour designs.

# CREASOUND

**Pop Electronique**
Cecil Leuter
Creasound re-badging. (JG)

**Informatic 2000**
Roger Roger and George Teperino
Futuristic synth work c.1982. (FM)

HISTORY: **Started in 1970, possibly as an extension of the classic french Neuilly library label.** OUTPUT: **Fairly extensive, covering all types of mood, with many licensed and re-badged recordings and pressings.** STYLE: **Mainly futuristic, progressive and electronic.** MUSICIANS OF NOTE: **Roger Roger, Nino Nardini, Jean Jacques Perrey.** SLEEVES: **From graphics to obscure photographic oddities and collages.**

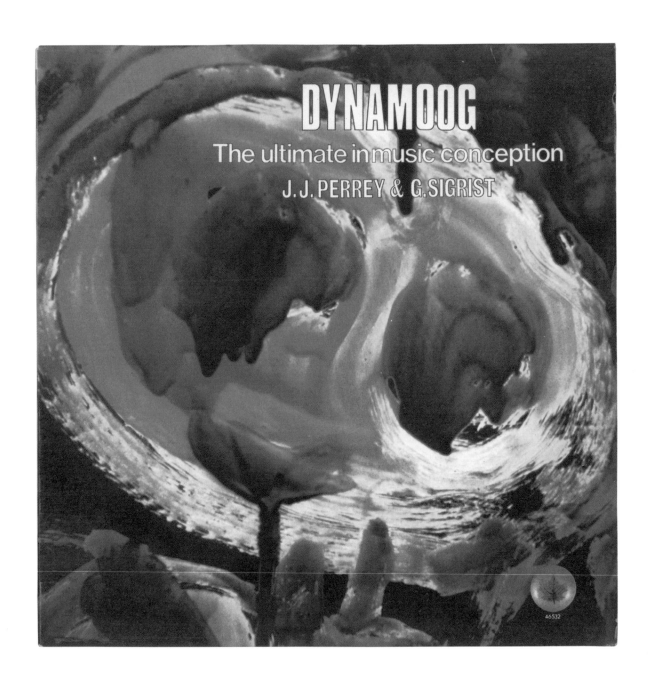

**Dynamoog**
J.J. Perrey and G. Sigrist
Experimental electronic moods. (JH)

# DE WOLFE

**TV Suite**
Peter Fenn and John Hawksworth
From cold stillness to disjointed fear. (I)

HISTORY: Hugely important independent label, founded in London in 1909. Library recordings originally recorded on 35mm open-track film, then later pressed on 78rpm, 10" 33rpm series began c.1960, then quickly moved into 12" 33rpm pressings. (See also Rouge, Hudson and Sylvester). OUTPUT: Vast number of regular pressings. Far reaching International distribution. Occasional sub-licensing from Musique Pour l'Image and Timing. STYLE: Themes and backgrounds covering every conceivable musical style. MUSICIANS OF NOTE: Alan Hawkshaw, Alan Parker, Nick Ingham, Jimmy Page, Basil Kirchin, Pete Reno, Johnny Hawksworth, Stanley Myers, Stephane Grappelli, Reg Tilsley, Stanley Black, Roger Webb. SLEEVES: Early 10" recordings have generic 'paper bag' style design with type variations. More illustrative designs continued throughout the 1970s and early-1980s. Long series of distinctive red house sleeves, and red / white / blue 'fanfare' sleeves. Early cover art by Rolph Webster, later 1970s sleeves mostly by Nick Bantock. FAMOUS CUES: 'The Gallery' from *Vision On*, various *Sweeney* dramatics, *Monty Python*, *Roobarb & Custard*, *Emmanuelle*, all *Dawn Of The Dead* incidentals, *Man About The House*, *Van der Valk*, *Witchfinder General* score.

**New Generation**
Laurence Stephen Orchestra
Modern sounds. (S)

**Journey Into Sound**
Light compositions with acoustic effects.
Early 'paper bag' style 10" sleeve. (JT)

**The Wild One**
Basil Kirchin's London studio group, Jimmy Page features.
10" release. (JT)

**High Speed Jazz**
Renaud and Gainsbourg International Jazz Group
10" release. (JT)

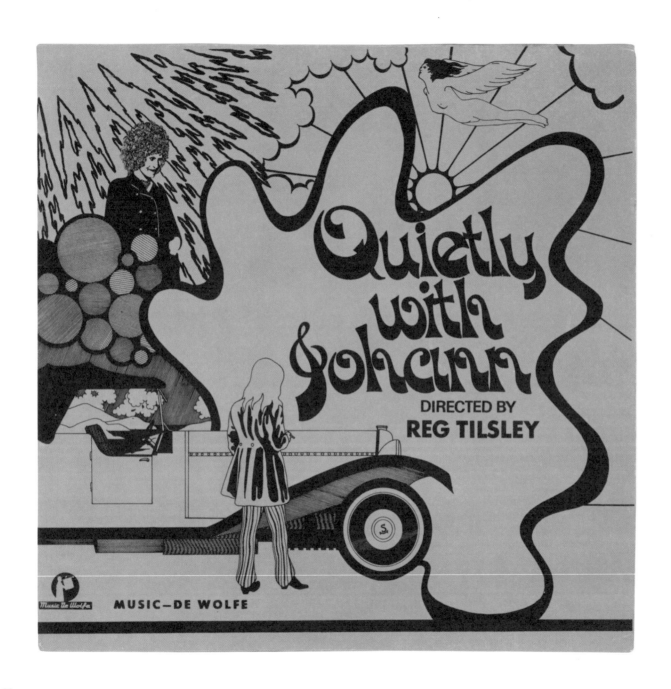

**Quietly with Johann**
Reg Tilsley
Classics and novelty pop.
10" release. (JT)

**Space Drive**
C. Evans-Ironside
Futuristic concepts. (MG)

**Push Button**
Contemporary electronic cues.
Sleeve by Kate Kelly. (MG)

**Rubber Riff**
Line-up features part of the band Soft Machine.
Modern rock. (JM)

**Dangerous Connection**
Drama, action, suspense. Small group sounds. (JM)

**Feeling High**
The Barry Stoller Band
Funky group sounds. (JM)

**Weekend World**
Simon Park
Dramatic themes. (JD)

**Hogan, The Hawk & Dirty John Crown**
Alan Parker and W. Parrish
Up to date group sounds. (JM)

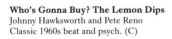

**Who's Gonna Buy? The Lemon Dips**
Johnny Hawksworth and Pete Reno
Classic 1960s beat and psych. (C)

**Z Patrol**
Reg Tilsley
Tough crime jazz. (C)

**Forest of Evil**
The Slipstream Group
Early synthesizer and drum machine cues, foreboding themes. (C)

**Even More Electric Banana**
Includes members of The Pretty Things.
Third LP in the Banana Series.
1960s beat and hard psych with vocals. (C)

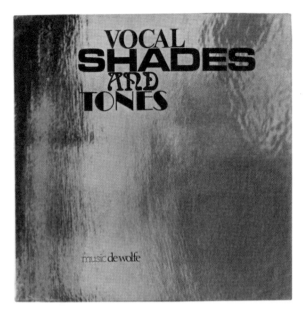

**Vocal Shades and Tones**
Barbara Moore
Classic scat LP. (JT)

**Sing Me A Song by Soft-Slipper**
Vocal and instrumental moods. (FM)

**Band 8**
Herbert Chappell
Small band novelties. (JT)

**Metal Sunrise**
P. Avray
Continental small group sounds. (FM)

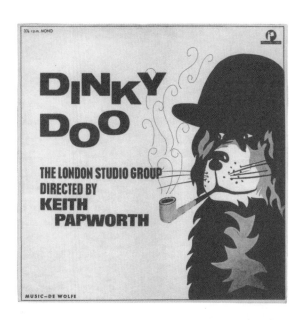

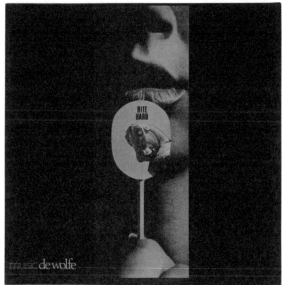

**A Rose For Dracula**
C. Staker
Dark horror and drama. (JM)

**Bite Hard**
Johnny Hawksworth
Powerful modern sounds. (JM)

**Dinky Doo**
Keith Papworth and the London Studio Group
Early and happy novelties. (LV)

**Highlight**
Hugo De Groot
Small group impressions. 10" release. (JT)

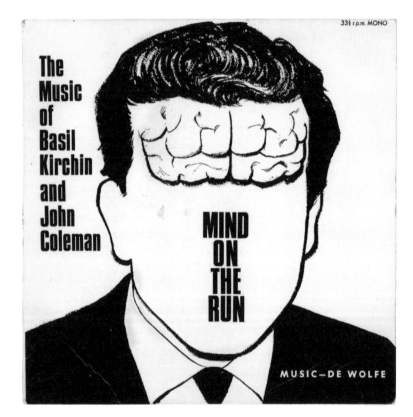

**Mind On The Run**
Basil Kirchin and John Coleman
Paranoid links and bridges. 10" release. (JT)

**New Decade**
The London Studio Group
Fine dramatics. (JM)

**Sun High**
Simon Park
Modern synthesizer dramatics. (JM)

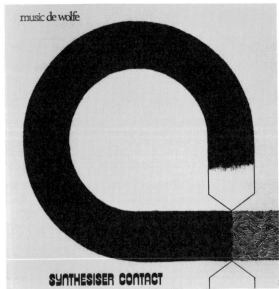

**8 Days A Week**
The Unit Seven Band
Easy going backgrounds. (JM)

**Synthesiser Contact**
Pete Reno
Modern small group sounds. (JM)

**Black Pearl**
Alan Hawkshaw and Alan Parker
Soulful, pacey and fresh sounds. (MG)

**Output**
Small orchestral, industrial sounds. (JM)

# DISC GO

**Go Go** Volume 1
J. C. Pierric and M. Chadcar (JD)

HISTORY: Italian, late-1970s. OUTPUT: Very small, possibly less than ten issues. STYLE: Standard commercial dramatics for the period. SLEEVES: Odd graphics and paintings.

mostra collettiva

**Mostra Collettiva**
Various artists
Various styles from jazz to drama. 1972. (JT)

HISTORY: Rome based label, from the early-1960s. OUTPUT: Above average number of releases. Very limited distribution, perhaps Italian only. Extremely limited pressings, now rare. STYLE: Jazz, bossa styles, some drama, romantic, religious. MUSICIANS OF NOTE: Possibly all pseudonyms. SLEEVES: Early sleeves green or black with simple stave design. Later issues use simple graphics and paintings. Unusually heavy card.

# EDI-PAN

**Imieiamici**
Bruno Nicolai
Themes of a zoo-like nature. (PW)

**Tempo sospeso**
Bruno Nicolai
Fuzz guitar led thriller and horror themes. 'Giallo' style. (C)

HISTORY: Mid-1970s label started by Bruno Nicolai, based in Rome. OUTPUT: Limited but regular. Some documentary soundtracks issued as library. STYLE: Odd, experimental, dark and brooding themes, travel and conflict a speciality. MUSICIANS OF NOTE: Leo Flag (Bruno Nicolai), Fred Bongusto. SLEEVES: Mostly photographic, some montages.

# EMBER

**MOOD MUSIC LIBRARY**

MOOD MUSIC LIBRARY

RECORD NUMBER ERL 3365

12-inch 33 r.p.m. long play album

**EMBER MOOD MUSIC
RECORDED LIBRARY**

for the use of

*Television, Film and Radio
Producers
Advertising Agencies*

To choose music for setting of scenes for visual and
background music on radio, television and films, etc.

**2000 Weeks**
Don Burrows
Jazz moods.
Rare Australian soundtrack issued as library. 1969. (SS)

HISTORY: Part of the large Ember music label, London, mid-1960s. OUTPUT: Small range of 12", 33rpm LPs. Many UK and international recordings licensed for library use. Poor pressing quality on some releases. STYLE: A random mixture, some impressive jazz. MUSICIANS OF NOTE: Tommy Whittle, Tubby Hayes. SLEEVES: Generic blue.

# EPERVIER

**Travelling** Volume 1
André Lutereau, The Travelling Orchestra.
Jazz themes. (JT)

**Travelling Flash**
André Lutereau
Various strings, skits and percussion. (JD)

HISTORY: Paris based label started c.1970. OUTPUT: Above average size release rate with sporadic international distribution. STYLE: Mainly small group sessions, everything from jazz to circus themes, with travel a speciality. MUSICIANS OF NOTE: André Lutereau, Michel Lorin. SLEEVES: Early sleeves with photographic distortions, later sleeves using colour graphics and photography. No distinctive house style. Early releases used photographs of artists on reverse.

# FAMA

**Suoni Di Una Citta'** Nuovaserie No.1
Teresa Luciani
Ambient and textured found sound. (C)

HISTORY: Obscure library offshoot of RCA Italy, c.1972 (see also Jubal).  OUTPUT: Very low with limited distribution. Now rare.  STYLE: Experimental, jazz, electronics, concrete.
SLEEVES: Photographic distortions.

# FLOWER

**Drammatico Per Quartetto D'Archi**
Paolo Renosto
Simple drama cues. (JT)

HISTORY: Independent Rome based label, part of Octopus. OUTPUT: Limited pressings. Possibly licensed from other small libraries. STYLE: Jazz themes, electronics, suspense and classical dramatics. SLEEVES: Generic style using type with colour variations.

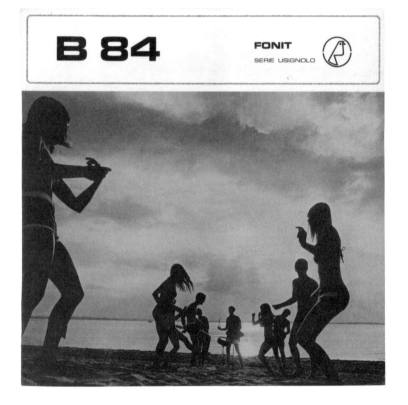

**B 84 New Sounds** (B Series)
Fabio Fabor
Jazz, bossas, includes *Bossa 7+*. (JT)

**C 267 Caratteristici** (C Series)
Giampiero Boneschi and Mitridate
Various experimental electronics. (JT)

HISTORY: Italian music giant with impressive library imprint. OUTPUT: Vast international catalogue with many pressings. Also some international sub-licensing and possibly smaller offshoots, (see Goldfinger). STYLE: From early traditional recordings to world music, classic mood themes and advanced electronics. MUSICIANS OF NOTE: Fabio Fabor, Giampiero Boneschi. SLEEVES: Illustrative, photographic and painted – spin paintings a favourite. Many specialist series.

UST 701 (UST Series)
Various artists
Ceremonial and religious music. (S)

**7002** (International Series)
Various artists
World music and folkloric. (S)

**7004** (International Series)
Various artists
Solo instruments and vocals. (S)

# FONOVIDEO

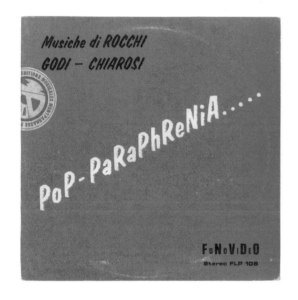

**PoP-PaRaPhReNiA.....**
Rocchi and Godi
Fine psych and pop. MP2000 sub-license sticker. (JG)

**Woman's Colours**
The Barigozzi Group
Pop jazz themes. (JG)

HISTORY: Italian, Rome based, started late-1960s. OUTPUT: Varied, possibly licensed and distributed in Italy through Vedette, with further international distribution through Montparnasse 2000. STYLE: Mood music from easy to pop, specialising in jazz. MUSICIANS OF NOTE: Most artists under pseudonyms. SLEEVES: Two or three-colour graphics.

# FREESOUND

**Understood**
Jacky Giordano and Robert Hermel
Includes *The faded charm of father sax*. 1973. (S)

**Ovation**
Various artists
Jazz, rock, electronics and more. 1973. (S)

HISTORY: Classic French label, founded in Paris in 1973. Part of the Ambient Musicale Illustration Sonore and in the UK associated with Harmonic and Studio G. OUTPUT: Limited number of releases. Few Freesound LPs exist, most are of a consistently high quality. Now rare. STYLE: Free, jazz based, artistic and dramatic. MUSICIANS OF NOTE: Jacky Giordano. SLEEVES: Collage on early issues.

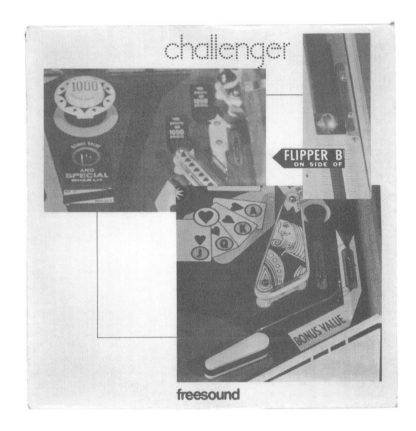

**Challenger**
Jacky Giordano
Percussion, electronics. 1974. (S)

**Schifters**
Jacky Giordano and Yan Tregger
Wah-wah and more. 1974. (S)

**Philopsis**
Jacky Giordano
Mechanical marches and drums, 1975. (S)

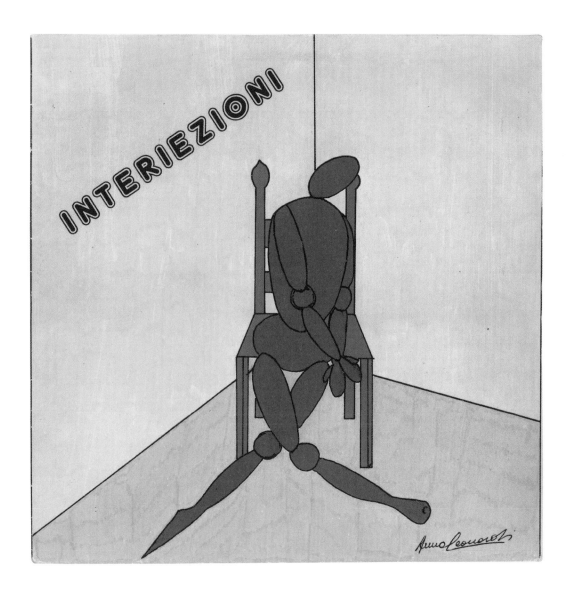

**Interiezioni**
L. Sordini (possibly Guiliano Sorgini). (JD)

HISTORY: Italian, Rome based, early-1970s, possibly associated with Squirrel (sic).  OUTPUT: Limited, now rare.  STYLE: Mainly experimental dramatics.  MUSICIANS OF NOTE: Artists mostly used pseudonyms.  SLEEVES: Simple graphics and typography.

# GEMELLI

**Voix**
Egisto Macchi
Ecrie treated choral vocals. (C)

**Contro Fase**
Ennio Morricone
Experimental, treated piano, electronics. (JT)

HISTORY: Independent label from 1970. Owned by Bruno Nicolai. OUTPUT: Limited catalogue. Some original scores. Very high quality pressings. STYLE: Mainly dark and experimental, some electronics. MUSICIANS OF NOTE: Ennio Morricone, Bruno Nicolai. SLEEVES: Hard-card sleeves with rich and varied graphics, photography and typography. Regular variations of logo.

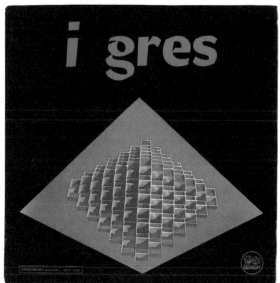

**Rendez Vous**
Bruno Nicolai
Dark, brooding, urban jazz themes. (JT)

**I Gres** Volume 2
Lo Turco and Rizzati
Various jazz themes. (JT)

**Espressioni**
Bruno Nicolai
Moody dramatics. (JT)

**Insight Modulation**
Zanagoria
Dark jazz. (I)

# GOLDEN RING

**Turn On**
Frank Mantis Group
Fine contemporary sounds. (JG)

**Orion 2000**
Pete Thomas
Classic 1975 recording. (JD)

HISTORY: Mid-1970s German based label, started by Ralph Marco. Possibly licensed internationally by Telemusic. OUTPUT: Average sized catalogue (see also Happy Records). STYLE: Mixture of obvious and classic library styles, from ragtime to love thematics. MUSICIANS OF NOTE: **Pete Thomas**. SLEEVES: Basic graphics and typography. Some unusual branded inner sleeves.

Golden Ring Records
A 30 012 RM Stereo

Make Friends

RALPH MARCO BAND

**Make Friends**
Ralph Marco Band
Unusual twisted beat themes. (JG)

# GOLDFINGER

**UST 335**
Guiliano Sorgini
Fine dramatics. Some percussion. (GJ)

HISTORY: Obscure label from Italy, possibly an offshoot of the giant Fonit library label.  OUTPUT: Average size. Limited distribution.  STYLE: Experimental, dramatic oddities.
MUSICIANS OF NOTE: Guiliano Sorgini.  SLEEVES: Similar in style and graphics to Fonit releases.

# GRIFO

SIGNORI:

L'ORCHESTRA!

GRIFO records
gr 516 mono

**Signori: l'Orchestra!**
Includes Sorgini, Fusco and Funaro
Simple classical cues. (JT)

HISTORY: Italian independent label, from the late-1960s to the early-1970s. OUTPUT: Very few issues traced, now scarce. STYLE: Diverse, specialising in classical themes.
MUSICIANS OF NOTE: Guiliano Sorgini. SLEEVES: Miscellaneous artwork.

**Mister Marco's Music**
Ralph Marco Band
Various contemporary mood cues. (GJ)

HISTORY: German label, part of the medium sized Golden Ring musical empire. OUTPUT: Very small. Limited distribution. Few releases traced. Rare. STYLE: Simple moods. Some good experimental jazz. MUSICIANS OF NOTE: Ralph Marco and his Band. SLEEVES: Simple graphics. Some letraset.

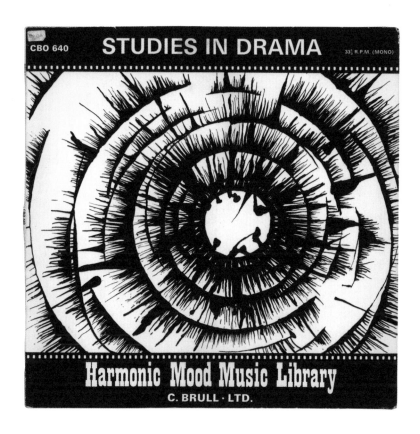

**Studies in Drama**
Martin Bottcher and Pete Thomas
Harmonic paint splatter sleeve. (JT)

**Music For Effect**
H. Possega
10" release. (JT)

HISTORY: London based, established in the mid-1960s. Part of the diverse Brull organisation. All releases have Brull catalogue numbers. OUTPUT: Some original sessions, many internationally licensed recordings (see Fonit), on 10" and 12". STYLE: Many releases have a strong jazz and experimental feel. MUSICIANS OF NOTE: Ronnie Ross, Burt Kaempfert. SLEEVES: Generic film strip sleeve on early 10" and 12" issues. Later LPs with standard orange house bag or paint splatter sleeve in various colourways.

# HIBOU

FANTASTIQUE SUSPENS ANGOISSE

PRODUCTIONS ET ÉDITIONS HIBOU

ETRANGE ESPACE MYSTERE

VOL.1

Hibou Volume 1
Philippe Bréjean
Suspense and mystery themes. (JH)

HISTORY: Productions et éditions Hibou, Paris late-1960s onwards. Hibou translates as 'Owl'. OUTPUT: Medium sized, however releases are scarce. STYLE: All dramatic and classic library music. SLEEVES: Simple wise owl graphic, book titles changed on each recording. Colour variations. Artwork by Héléne Courtaigne.

# HOMERE

**Homere Instrumental**
Jean Michel Lorgere
Modern compositions. (JG)

**Karaté K.** No. 1
Pierre Louvet
Progressive jazz sounds. (JG)

HISTORY: Known as Homere Instrumental, this is a small Paris based label from the late-1960s. OUTPUT: Small but well documented. There are eighteen traceable LP releases, plus a further unusual ten single 7" issues. STYLE: Everything from straight jazz to classical and some more experimental releases. SLEEVES: Simple, graphics. Some collage.

**Magnum**
Artwork by Ian Tregger,
(music possibly by Jan Tregger). (JH)

# HUDSON

**Headline**
Barbara Moore
Modern orchestral pieces. (JD)

**Mindbender**
Avant-jazz.
Artwork by Ken Hutchinson Associates. (JM)

HISTORY: Company started in London, mid-1930s, producing strict tempo dance music. Acquired by De Wolfe Music which produced library LPs from around 1965 onwards.
OUTPUT: Medium sized catalogue, internationally distributed. STYLE: Fine mood music, electronics, jazz, experimentals. SLEEVES: As with later De Wolfe catalogue, graphics, freestyle illustration and photography. FAMOUS CUES: *Dawn Of The Dead* incidentals.

# L'ILLUSTRATION MUSICALE
## (IM)

IM 26

IM 26 **Organ Plus**
Jacky Giordano
Generic sleeve. (S)

HISTORY: L'Illustration Musicale, Paris based label started as a publishing house by jazz pianist Eddie Warner in the late-1960s. OUTPUT: Library issues began c.1970. Only twenty-six releases. STYLE: Jazz, experimental, quirky, electronic. MUSICIANS OF NOTE: Eddie Warner, Jacky Giordano, Johnny Hawksworth, Roger Roger. SLEEVES: Generic 'im' sleeves, some house bags. Different colourways. Simple logos with various graphic treatments. Sparse sleevenotes.

IM 25 **Sound Industrial**
Roger Roger (JD)

IM 22 **Cops, Crooks and Spies**
Eddie Warner
Classic experimentals. (JD)

# ILLER

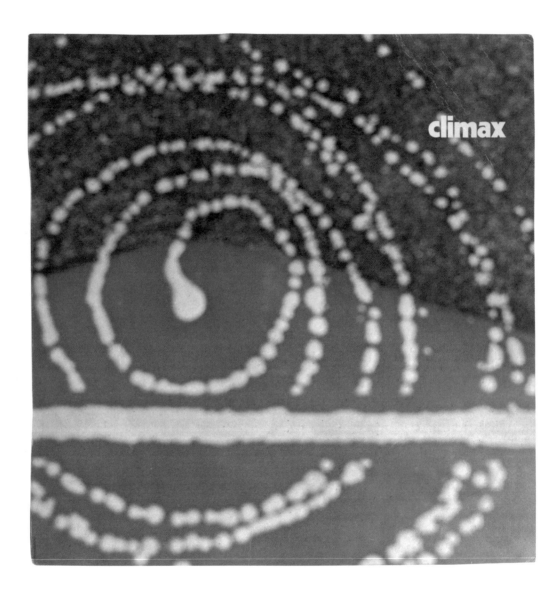

**Climax** Issue 1
Marega
Way out electronics. (JT)

HISTORY: Obscure Italian label affiliated with RCA Italy. First issues 1971, (see also Jubal). OUTPUT: Very small. Now rare. STYLE: Experimental, electronics, percussion.
MUSICIANS OF NOTE: Most artists worked under pseudonyms. SLEEVES: Photographic.

# IML
## (INTERNATIONAL MUSIC LABEL)

IML 02 **Drumo Vocalo**
Daniel Humair
Drums, vocals, special effects. (JH)

IML 04 **Hypnose**
Teddy Lasry
Dark, hypnotic sounds. (JD)

HISTORY: Paris based from early-1970s. Subsidiary of the Montparnasse label. OUTPUT: Small, internationally licensed recordings. STYLE: Experimental, avant-garde, uneasy listening, progressive. MUSICIANS OF NOTE: Teddy Lasry, Daniel Humair, Bernard Lubat. SLEEVES: IML logo always prominent. Various graphic and photographic styles.

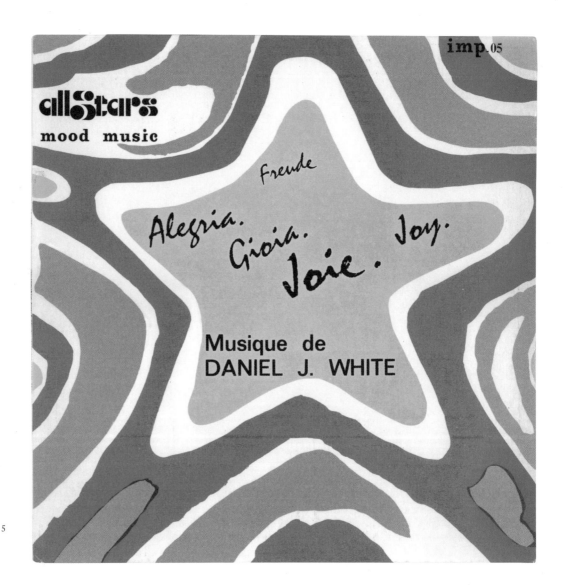

**All Stars Mood Music Selection** IMP 5
Daniel J. White
Simple mood and pop sounds.
Includes *Naked Dames In Fur*. (JT)

HISTORY: Paris based library, dating from 1972. OUTPUT: Small. Very limited European distribution. Now rare. STYLE: Pop and easy moods. MUSICIANS OF NOTE: Daniel White.
SLEEVES: Bright, simple graphics.

# IMPRESS

IMPRESS

GUT REACTION!

COMPOSER
DUNCAN LAMONT

IA 421

**Gut Reaction!**
Duncan Lamont
Fast, repetitive rhythms and moods. (S)

HISTORY: Early London based label, an acronym of Inter-art Music Publishers, who worked in TV, theatre, radio and motion picture productions. Acquired by Joseph Weinberger in the mid-1950s. OUTPUT: Large catalogue on 78rpm, moving into 33rpm production in the early-1960s. STYLE: Fine dramatics. MUSICIANS OF NOTE: Trevor Duncan, Duncan Lamont. SLEEVES: Early 10" in plain white sleeves. 12" LPs in distinctive blue and white block pattern.

# JUBAL

music specially recorded for film, radio and television

**Tastiere**
Paolo Ormi (legendary arranger).
Repetitive percussion and moog sounds. (JT)

HISTORY: Obscure small Italian label from Rome, c.1970. Experimental library and part of the RCA empire (which also includes Fama, Iller, and Fono Film). OUTPUT: Brief lifespan with small number of releases. Limited Italian only distribution. Now rare. STYLE: Jazz, electronics, percussion, repetitive cues. MUSICIANS OF NOTE: Paolo Ormi. SLEEVES: Simple typography, one-colour only.

# JOSEPH WEINBERGER
## (JW MEDIA MUSIC)

JW 401

BOB DOWNES' NEW SOUNDS

for FLUTE, PERCUSSION and SYNTHESIZER

JW 401

THEME MUSIC

**Bob Downes' New Sounds**
Percussive, exotic, eastern, avant-garde. (JT)

HISTORY: Legendary label, originating in Austria in 1884 as a publisher of musical theatre. UK company incorporated in 1937. Earliest recordings for Weinberger's Theme Music label dating from around 1956. Shortly after it acquired the Inter Art Music company who owned the Impress label. Later a third company and label was created, Background Music Publishers 'Audio' label, producing a further thirty LPs. OUTPUT: Medium sized catalogue from early 78rpm issues to 12" 33rpm. MUSICIANS OF NOTE: Ronald Binge, Trevor Duncan, Desmond Leslie, Sydney Dale, Bob Downes, Pete Thomas. SLEEVES: Early vinyl 12" releases with white and yellow block patterns. Moving to plain light brown sleeves in late-1970s. FAMOUS CUES: *Screen Test* theme, *9 O'Clock News* theme, *Plan 9 From Outer Space* incidentals.

# KPM

The classic KPM 1000 Series.
Generic green sleeve. (JT)

Standard KPM Series, burnt orange sleeve.
Pre-1000 Series and repressed 78rpm recordings. (JT)

HISTORY: Roots can be traced to Robert Keith, London 1780. Library recordings on 78rpm pressed from 1955. Green 1000 series began 1965, initiated by Robin Phillips. OUTPUT: Internationally renowned recordings, world wide distribution, massive vinyl pressings and vast catalogue. MUSICIANS OF NOTE: Brian Bennett, John Cameron, Alan Parker, Keith Mansfield, Johnny Pearson, Francy Boland, Neil Ardley, Syd Dale, Ron Geesin. SLEEVES: From the earliest 78rpm recordings are reissues in the standard numbered series in burnt orange sleeves, followed by the generic KPM olive green 1000 series sleeve, with accidental variations in tone. Early 1000 LPs have large and small cube system for titles on the reverse. Late-1970s saw graphic devises and full colour artwork. FAMOUS CUES: *Mastermind*, *Captain Pugwash*, *Deep Throat* incidentals, *News At Ten*, *Wicker's World*.

# LEO

**Percussioni In Crescendo**
Guiliano Sorgini (JG)

HISTORY: Very obscure Italian label, late-1960s to early-1970s. Possibly Rome based. OUTPUT: Small mix of licensed and original recordings. STYLE: Dramatic electronics, percussion, experimentals. MUSICIANS OF NOTE: Giampiero Boneschi, Guiliano Sorgini. SLEEVES: Simple effective graphics.

**Carosello Musicale**
Evasio Roncarati and Gino Mescoli
Various compositions. (JD)

**America Giovane**
R. Ducros
Italy meets electric America. (S)

HISTORY: Independent Italian label based in Rome, early-1970s onwards. OUTPUT: Sporadic releases. Early issues now rare. STYLE: Italian jazz / rock with an American bias. Some original scores issued. SLEEVES: From simple typography to painted and photographic artwork.

# LIUTO

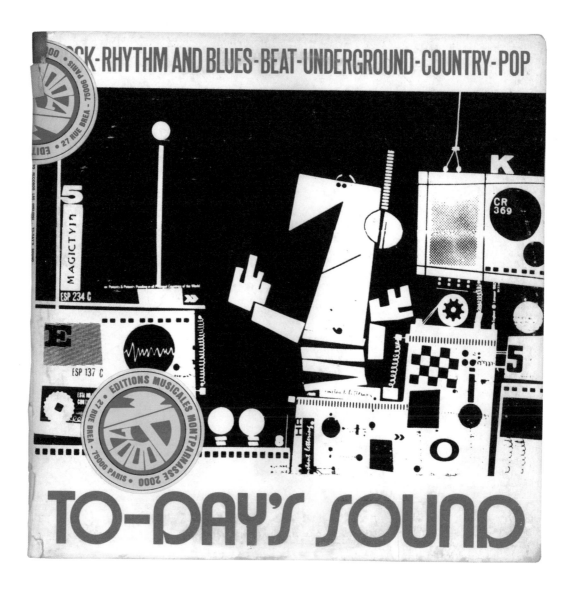

**To-day's Sound**
Umiliani and the Soundworshippers
MP 2000 distribution stickers. (JG)

HISTORY: Composer Piero Umiliani's own Italian label. Started in Rome, late-1960s. Also affiliated with Sound Workshop. Both library and soundtrack recordings issued. OUTPUT: Prolific, possibly assisted by RCA distribution and pressing. Some international distribution via MP 2000. STYLE: Filmic and thematic, experimental and electronics, jazzy concepts. High standard of musicianship. MUSICIANS OF NOTE: Piero Umiliani and his own pseudonyms. SLEEVES: Various styles. Collage, photography and graphics.

# LUPUS

**Impressioni Musicali**
Paride Miglioli
A diverse mixture of styles, from traditional to grotesque. (S)

**Colori Bozzetti E Miniature Musicali**
Paride Miglioli
Experimental music. (S)

HISTORY: Prolific label from Italy, c.1973. OUTPUT: High rate of LP production for international distribution. Original compositions and some sub-licensing to Sonimage. STYLE: Broad range, some rare vocals in the Telemusica Series. MUSICIANS OF NOTE: Mostly pseudonyms. SLEEVES: No generic feel, but consistently simple and effective artwork.

**Telemusica** No. 6
Various artists
Easy, jazz. (JG)

**Psycheground**
Ninety
Psychedelic sounds. (JG)

ITALIA MINIMA ITALIA MINIMA ITA
LIA MINIMA ITALIA MINIMA ITALIA
MINIMA ITALIA MINIMA ITALIA MIN
NIMA ITALIA MINIMA ITALIA MINIM
A ITALIA MINIMA ITALIA MINIMA I
TALIA MINIMA ITALIA MINIMA ITAL
IA MINIMA ITALIA MINIMA ITALIA A
MINIMA ITALIA MINIMA ITALIA MIN
IMA ITALIA MINIMA ITALIA MINIMA
A ITALIA MINIMA ITALIA MINIMA IT
ALIA MINIMA ITALIA MINIMA ITALI
A ITALIA MINIMA ITALIA MINIMA I
TALIA MINIMA ITALIA MINIMA ITAL
IA MINIMA ITALIA MINIMA ITALIA A
MINIMA ITALIA MINIMA ITALIA MIN

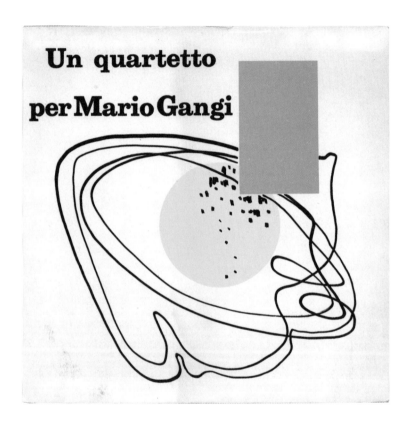

**Italia Minima**
Sordini and Casa
Various dramatics. (S)

**Un quartetto per Mario Gangi**
Radici
Classical cues. (JT)

**Tempo Di Naja**
Remigio Ducros
Dramatic jazz. (JT)

HISTORY: Very obscure Italian label from the early-1970s. No dates exist. OUTPUT: Approximately twenty LPs traced. Very little information available. STYLE: Jazzy and experimental. SLEEVES: Block colour and simple typography.

# MARCY MUSIC

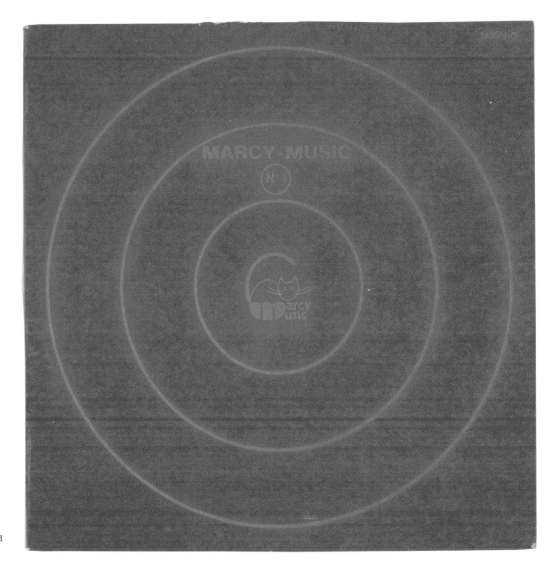

**Timing** No. 1
Piget, Batailley, Ztepczak, Jourdain and Rolland
Dreamy fusion. (C)

HISTORY: **Obscure mid 1970s French label. Distributed by C. Brull in the UK.** OUTPUT: **Very small. Possibly under ten releases.** STYLE: **Experimental mood music from various composers.** SLEEVES: **Simple cat graphic.**

MARIGNAN

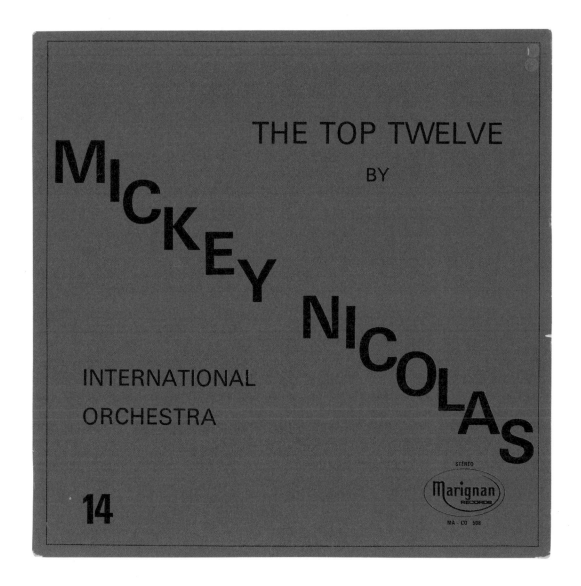

THE TOP TWELVE

BY

MICKEY NICOLAS

INTERNATIONAL

ORCHESTRA

14

STÉRÉO

Marignan
RECORDS

MA - CO 508

**The Top Twelve** No. 14
Mickey Nicolas
Up-tempo jazz. (JG)

HISTORY: **Late-1960s Paris based label.** OUTPUT: **Small and very poor distribution. Little documentation or history available. Rare.** STYLE: **From classics to pop melodies and jazz.** SLEEVES: **Basic two-colour.**

**Blended (Melodies)**
Michael Maller
Easy jazz. (JG)

HISTORY: Independent label based in Paris, c.1968.   OUTPUT: Very small. Possibly only ten releases. Now rare.   STYLE: Melodic themes, jazz and easy.   SLEEVES: Simple two colour graphics.

# MONDIOPHONE

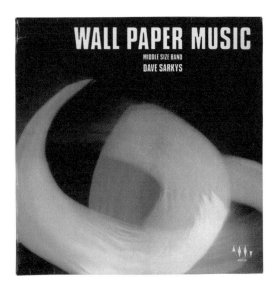

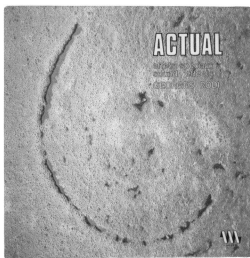

**Wall Paper Music**
Dave Starkys
Instrumental and vocal sounds. (FM)

**Actual**
Georges Rodi
Psychedelic sounds. (JD)

**SO4H2**
Michel Gonet
Modern moods. (JD)

**Eve For Ever**
Michel Gonet
Vocal jazz group sounds. (FM)

HISTORY: Large Paris based organisation started in the late-1960s.  OUTPUT: Extensive international pressings. Sub-licensing worldwide.  STYLE: All styles, genres and moods comprehensively covered.  MUSICIANS OF NOTE: Michel Gonet, Janko Nilovic, Micheline Ramette.  SLEEVES: Photographic manipulations.

DOWN
IN THE
CITY N° 1

**Down In The City** No. 1
Franco Potenza
Urban jazz, small group. (SS)

HISTORY: Bizarre, totally obscure Italian label, possibly early-1970s.　OUTPUT: Very small and scarce. Little information available.　STYLE: Simple jazz-based recordings.
SLEEVES: Unusual designs including felt-tip pen.

# MONTPARNASSE 2000

## (MP2000)

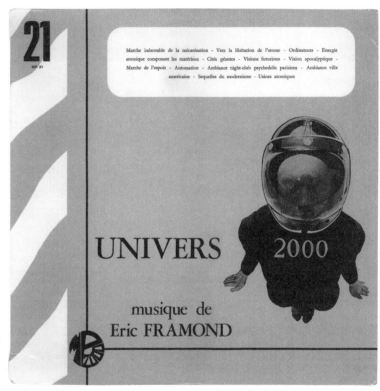

13. **Monologue Pour**
Daniel White
Solo instruments. (JT)

21. **Univers 2000**
Eric Framond
Satan meets jazz. (C)

HISTORY: One of the great, prolific labels from Paris, established as a music label but moved into library music from 1968 until the mid-1970s. Label started by Andre Farry, assisted by Louis Delacour (aka Pepe Luis). Small offshoot label called St Germain Des Prés. OUTPUT: Large and consistent, with regular repressings. MUSICIANS OF NOTE: Daniel White, Janko Nilovic, Eric Framond. SLEEVES: Highly distinctive. Unique flag design which continues on spine. Early releases used illustrations and photography, these changed to block colours for represses.

La parade des pantins - La forêt enchantée - Le Texas à l'heure de l'électronique - Tea for two - L'époque de la prohibition - Bistrot des années 20 - Jazzmen en liberté - Souper aux chandelles - Les grands ensembles - Coup d'envoi - Ambiance orientale - Climat tropical - Rythme fascinant de la bossa-nova - Ambiance début des années 30 - Mélodie romantique - Réunion familiale

STYLISSIMO

**40. Stylissimo**
Camille Sauvage and Jerry Mengo
Electronic madness. (LV)

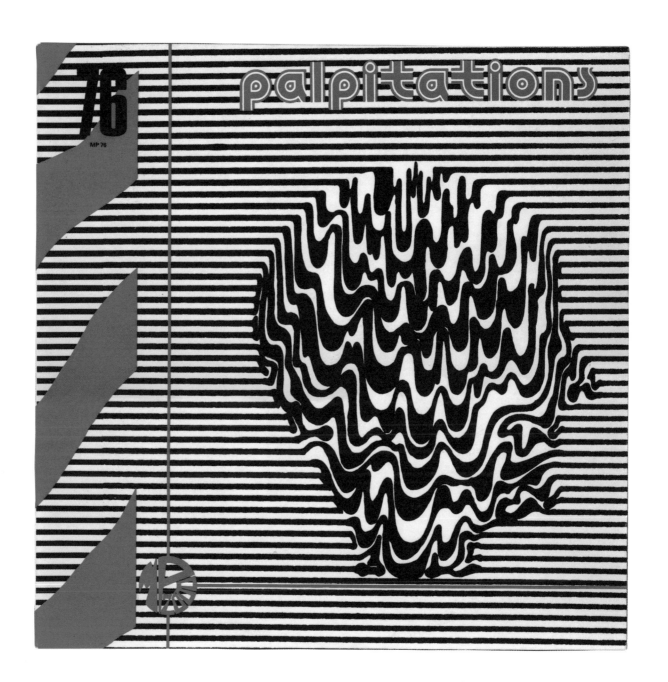

**76. Palpitations**
Eric Framond
Twisted jazz themes. (JG)

25. **Moog Sensations**
J.J. Perrey and P. Prilly
Fast boogie to slow foxtrot, in moog. (JM)

68. **Puzzle** Actualities Series
Eric Framond
Pop / sports. (JM)

**84. Un Homme Dans l'Univers**
Janko Nilovic
Keyboard led easy listening. (C)

**6. Psyc' Impressions**
Janko Nilovic
Deranged, guitar led psychedelia. (C)

**46. Musique A Show**
Eric Framond
Classical / progressive with heavy percussion. (C)

**33. Fantasmagories**
Camille Sauvage
Horror themes, percussive abstract fusion. (C)

**MUSIC**
the food of life

96
MP 96

96. **Music the food of life**
The Jack Dieval's Sextet
Modern jazz themes. (JM)

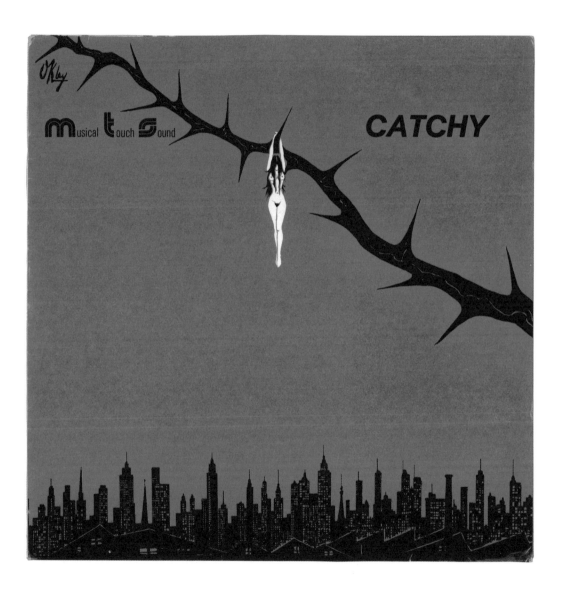

**Catchy**
Yan Tregger
Disco moods. Artwork by Oklay. (S)

HISTORY: Obscure independent label started in 1976. Paris based. Possibly owned by Yan Tregger. OUTPUT: Very few releases traced, possibly less than ten. STYLE: Electronics with a lively feel, moving into disco and fantasy cues. SLEEVES: One or two colour illustrations, simple, weird.

**Unusual Beat Sounds Fantasy**
Giampiero Boneschi
Dance, electronic and moody themes.
TRF distribution sticker. (LV)

HISTORY: Prolific Italian library label, c.1970, subsidiary of Jump Records. OUTPUT: Very large but inconsistent. International licensing. STYLE: A mixture of classic and mood music cues and some experimental electronics. MUSICIANS OF NOTE: Giampiero Boneschi. SLEEVES: Earlier sleeves have simple green and white typography. Later pressings have scientific photography.

**Musik Mosaik** Volume 3
Bottcher and Kuhn
Musical experiments. (JD)

HISTORY: German label, Hamburg based, mid to late-1970s. No precise dates available. OUTPUT: Very small, hard to trace. Now rare. STYLE: Jazz based, experimentals.
SLEEVES: Simple sparse graphics.

# MUSIQUE POUR L'IMAGE

MPI. No. 34. **Musique de Enfance**
Vladimir Cosma
Electro-medieval sounds. (JT)

MPI. No. 22. **Action**
Martial Solal
Fine jazz for action. (JT)

HISTORY: Important Paris based label, started by pianist and jazz composer Robert Viger. Began issuing 10" recordings c.1968, changing to 12" LPs after twenty issues. OUTPUT: Small to medium sized catalogue but limited output in terms of units pressed. Rare and desirable recordings. Some sub-licensing to Sylvester. STYLE: A complete range from jazz dramatics to experimental and children's music. MUSICIANS OF NOTE: Geminiani, Vladimir Cosma, Claude Vasori, Martial Solal. SLEEVES: Stunning black and white graphics and photography, collages also. Most sleeves by Robert J. Hilton.

JAZZ MOBILE

N° 6

musique pour l'image

ROBERT J. HILTON

MPI. No. 6. **Jazz Mobile**
Henri Renaud, Robert Hermel, Martial Solal
Fine jazz.
Sleeve by Robert J. Hilton. (JH)

MPI. No. 5. **Espace et Actualité**
Patrice Sciortino, Claude Vasori, François Bayle
Sleeve by Robert J. Hilton. (JH)

MPI. No. 26. **Guitares Rythmes et Guitares**
Roger Davey
1970. Sleeve by Robert J. Hilton. (JH)

MPI. No. 33. **Sons Nouveaux Pour Images Contemporaines**
Roger Davey
Various exotic, jazz and progressive themes. (JT)

MPI. No. 39. **Harlem Pop Trotters**
J. B. Raiteux
Improvised folk and more. (S)

MPI. No. 35. **Voyage Extraordinaire**
Vincent Geminiani
Art meets pop, jazz and percussion. (FM)

MPI. No. 38. **Infini**
Fabio Fabor, Armando Sciascia
Italian experiments. (SS)

MPI. No. 24. **Jazz Pour l'Action**
Richard Eldwyn
Fast and fine jazz themes. (JG)

MPI. No. 36. **Cocktail d'Images**
Claude Vasori (JG)

MPI. No. 27. **Ultra Popop**
Vladimir Cosma
Sleeve by Robert Planet. (JG)

MPI. No. 29. **Images en Movement**
Claude Vasori
Includes *Drug Pop*. Sleeve by Didier La Mache. (JG)

MPI. No. 2. **Action Charme Espace**
Claude Vasori
All jazz sounds. (JG)

**Musique Pour Le Futur**
Nino Nardini
Visionary electronics. (JD)

**Sports Plein Air**
Roger Roger
Creasound licensing sticker over Neuilly logo. (SS)

HISTORY: Early Paris based label, founded c.1965. OUTPUT: Average size, varied catalogue on 10" and 12", now scarce. Licensing to Creasound. STYLE: Jazz, experimentals, tribal sounds, electronics, scat. MUSICIANS OF NOTE: Roger Roger, The Jumping Jacques, Nino Nardini, Janko Nilovic. SLEEVES: Plain typographic 10" sleeves, with more decorative and illustrative 12" sleeves.

**Musique Idiote**
Roger Roger
Insane electronics. (LO)

**Jungle Obssession**
Nino Nardini and Roger Roger
Killer exotics. (FM)

New World W-23 / 24
Anonymous artist
Percussion and rock. (JT)

HISTORY: Mid-1970s, thematic library from Robert Hall Productions, 115 West 57th Street, New York. OUTPUT: Small and repetitive. Rare issues, possibly just twenty-five LPs. STYLE: Fairly sparse rhythmic tracks and themes. SLEEVES: Sleeveless. Possibly a house bag, but none have been traced to date.

**NIKE**

NIKE
NCM 1002
STEREOMONO COMPATIBILE

**TENSIONI**
**2**

**Tensioni** 2
Bruno Battisti
Hard and percussive drama cues. (JT)

HISTORY: Independent label based in Rome founded in 1971. OUTPUT: Very small. STYLE: Specialists in drama and tension themes. MUSICIANS OF NOTE: Bruno Battisti. SLEEVES: Generic house sleeve with number and title changes.

# OCTOPUS

**Telegiornale** Octopus 7
Atmo (aka Amedeo Tommasi)
Jazz and psychedelia. (JT)

**Clouds**
Lino and Castiglione
Funky jazz fusion. (SS)

HISTORY: Independent Italian label based in Rome, founded in the late-1960s. OUTPUT: Mainly Italy, low number of pressings, high quality music. Collectable. STYLE: Strong mixture of music, from heavy jazz to heavy dramatics, often with psychedelic fringes. Most vinyls pressed in the early-1970s have pressing fault on side one track one. MUSICIANS OF NOTE: Alessandro Alessandroni, Conrado, Montanari, frequent pseudonyms. SLEEVES: Early issues have a pink octopus on the sleeve, this changed to simple graphic type in later issues.

**Impacto** The Bigroup
Rock and funk.
Originally issued as Big Hammer on the Peer label. (S)

HISTORY: Small and obscure Spanish label from Barcelona, c.1974. OUTPUT: Possibly only in sub-licensing other library recordings from Europe. STYLE: Mainly rock and funk dramatics. SLEEVES: Bold graphics.

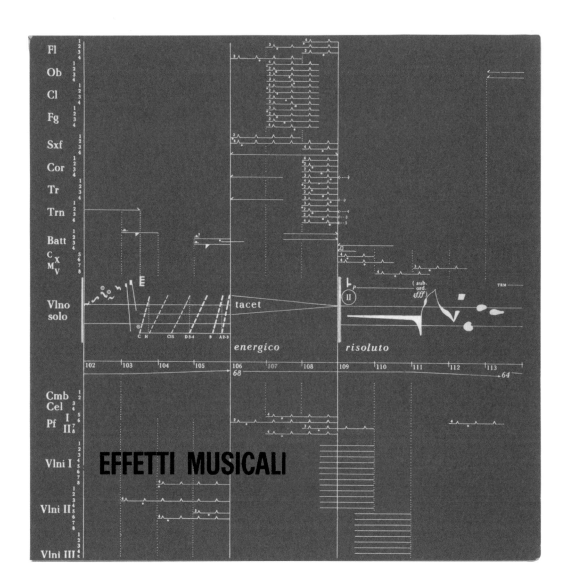

**Effetti Musicali** Sonorisation Series
Piero Umiliani
Experimental ambient electronics. (JT)

HISTORY: Rome based label, founded by Piero Umiliani in the late-1960s. Issued obscure soundtracks and music specifically for film and television. OUTPUT: Small and exceptionally rare. Desirable, hard to find LPs. STYLE: Experimental, easy, filmic. MUSICIANS OF NOTE: Piero Umiliani under various pseudonyms. SLEEVES: Graphic with photography for film releases.

# ORLY

**Mr. Diabolicus / Mr. Mysterious** Kaleidoscope No. 13.
Fabio Fabor
Hectic electronics from the Kaleidoscope Series. (JT)

HISTORY: Paris based label, c.1969. OUTPUT: Frequent with fairly large catalogue including some 7" vinyl. STYLE: Original French music and licensed experimentals from Italy. MUSICIANS OF NOTE: Giampiero Boneschi, Fabio Fabor. SLEEVES: Generic two-colour bordered sleeve. Also issued a long series of spin painting sleeves.

PARRY MUSIC

PML 37
PML 37

25.00

JOURNEY INTO SPACE

pm

parry music library    music for films, tv, radio

**Journey into Space**
Artus and Kass
Drama with electronics and synthesizers. (JD)

HISTORY: Label based in Toronto, Canada, late-1970s. OUTPUT: Fairly large catalogue. Sporadic international distribution, some by Studio G. STYLE: Mainly electronic and experimental, with a contemporary feel. MUSICIANS OF NOTE: Bunny J. Browne, Johnny Hawksworth, Roger Roger. SLEEVES: Standard numbered two-colour blue and white maple leaf design.

# PATCHWORK

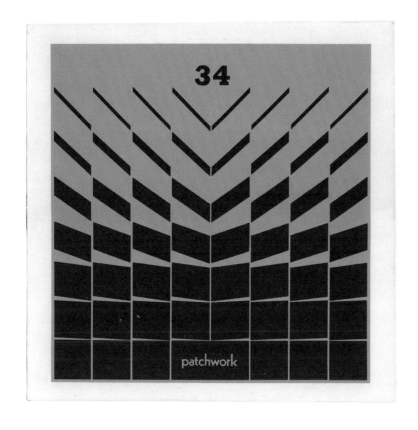

34. **Energie**
Claude Perraudin
Post disco conceptual electronics. (JT)

13.
Marc Chantereau / Delaporte
More electronics. (JD)

HISTORY: Mid-1970s Paris based label. OUTPUT: Large numbered catalogue. STYLE: Mainly electronic, conceptual and modern. MUSICIANS OF NOTE: Eric Demarsan, Guy Boulanger. SLEEVES: Generic design. Simple and dynamic colourways.

# PEER INTERNATIONAL LIBRARY LIMITED
## (PILL)

**Solar Flares**
Sven Libaek and his Orchestra
Space age vibey jazz. (S)

**Inter-Relation**
Johnny Scott and his Scottmen
Good jazz. 1970. (S)

HISTORY: Classic London label based in Denmark Street. Started c.1968. Affiliated with Southern, many titles appear across both labels. OUTPUT: Regular LPs, internationally distributed, but in fairly small numbers. Now scarce. STYLE: Jazz to classics, with a good range of electronics and progressive rock. MUSICIANS OF NOTE: Sven Libaek, Johnny Scott and the Scottmen, Nino Nardini. SLEEVES: Wide ranging styles, using photography and graphics. Distinctive and dynamic.

**Confrontation**
Frank Sterling Big Band
Large orchestrals. (SS)

**Five Plus Four** Powerhouse
Al Newman (S)

**Lost Star**
Memo
Includes *Filigree Funk*. 1978. (JM)

**Soul of a City**
Leonhardt and his Orchestra
Urban sounds. (SS)

Percussion Unit
**WORKFORCE**

**Workforce** Percussion Unit
Dramatic industrials.
Southern Library pressing. (S)

**Gemini** The Barrie Moore Combo
Anthony Mawer (SS)

**Scoop**
John Fiddy, Brain Dee, Clive Hicks
Dramatic and sporting themes. (S)

**Sweet Surprise**
Various artists
Classical strings. (JT)

**Electric Bazaar**
Anthony King
Electronics, toys, cats and storms. (S)

**Mind Bender**
Nino Nardini, Roger Roger, Forgie and Anthony Mawer
Legendary progressive pop sounds by Stringtronics. (MG)

**Sun-Seeker**
David Johnson
Guitar action. (MG)

**Flip Top**
Barrie Moore Combo
Various jazz moods. (MG)

**Point Blank**
Dorothy Lapelle
Panther formed for this recording only. (S)

**No Waiting**
Peter Dennis Orchestra
Light moods. (SS)

**Hangover**
Wolfgang Schlüter Combo
European jazz fusion. Artwork by Jack Mooring. (JT)

**String Scene**
Anthony Mawer Orchestra
Light orchestral and latin moods. 1970. (JM)

**My Thing**
Sven Libaek
Pop / jazz. Includes *Misty Canyon*. (JT)

**Earth Shaker**
Midas Touch
Romance / disco / marches. (S)

Photoplay
"Q"
Music Library

Stereo

**Q** Photoplay 13
Ronnie Hazlehurst
Various easy cues. (S)

HISTORY: Very small London label, based in St. John's Wood, c.1972. OUTPUT: A short-lived library issuing original sessions and some international licensing. STYLE: From easy listening to jazz quartets and big band compositions. MUSICIANS OF NOTE: Don Lusher and Ronnie Hazlehurst. SLEEVES: Generic red and white sleeve.

## PM
(PEGGY MONCLAIR)

**Music For Show** Volume 4
No artists named.
Brazilian themes and tangoes. (LV)

HISTORY: Early-1970s label from Paris.  OUTPUT: Small, rare recordings.  STYLE: Pop to jazz, with heavy focus on popular international rhythms.  MUSICIANS OF NOTE: Few named.  SLEEVES: Painted representations of a car.

**PONY**

33 XLP 10010
Stereomono

CAVALLARO '75

**DUE VOLTI: UNA MUSICA**

**Due Volti: Una Musica**
Various artists including Voodoo
Experimental cues. (JT)

HISTORY: Rome based library, c.1974 or 1975, affiliated with the larger Beat label. OUTPUT: Small number of releases, quite rare. STYLE: From classical cues to jazz.
MUSICIANS OF NOTE: Voodoo, Bonfanti. SLEEVES: Distinctive house look, red borders with varied illustrations by Cavallaro.

**Delta Sound**
J. C. Pierric
Jazz, funk and vocal harmonies. (JG)

HISTORY: Label based in Bezons, North West of Paris. OUTPUT: Very limited, exceptionally rare recordings. STYLE: Standard mood music melodies and rhythms. SLEEVES: Simple, using plain graphics and type. One colour artwork.

# PSI

**Minotaure** - Illustration 2
Christian Piget
Electronic and easy. (JT)

**Ionic Scrabble**
Claude Vasori
Experimental cues, repetitive rhythms. (SS)

HISTORY: A French label, based in Boulogne, early through to late-1970s. An offshoot of Musique Pour l'Image. OUTPUT: Medium sized library, regular releases. Licensed worldwide, normally via C. Brull. STYLE: Very conceptual style LPs, far from standard library recordings. MUSICIANS OF NOTE: Nancy Holloway, Manu Dibango, Martial Solal. SLEEVES: Graphics, collage, photography. No definitive house style.

**Dinha Mantha's Power**
Nancy Holloway (vocals)
Jazz, percussion, soul. (JT)

**Locomotion**
Martial Solal
Jazz forms. (C)

structures
percussions

**Structures Percussions**
Charles Bellonzi and Robert Vigier
Abstract percussion. (JH)

**The Hound Of Music**
Georges Arvanitas Quartet
Modal jazz numbers. (JG)

**African Voodoo**
Manu Dibango
Rare African themes. (JG)

**Chronoradial**
Patrice Sciortino
Avant-garde percussion. (JH)

## PROGRAMME MUSIC

**Shades of Rock**
Projection. Includes guitarist Rod Price
from Fog Hat. (JD)

HISTORY: Established in London in 1971 by Joseph Weinberger to supply the BBC's Coded Music service. OUTPUT: Twenty-six LPs, all recordings eventually incorporated into the Joseph Weinberger library catalogue. STYLE: Easy, jazz and rock, fine contemporary sounds. MUSICIANS OF NOTE: David Snell. SLEEVES: Generic purple with white type.

Q1
Kiessling and Peter Jaques, Orchestra Heuve
Jazz themes. (JG)

HISTORY: German label, dating from the early-1970s. Little traceable history. No sleevenotes or dates available.   OUTPUT: Very small, only a few releases.   STYLE: Jazz, big band.   MUSICIANS OF NOTE: Peter Jaques.   SLEEVES: One-colour graphics.

# RCA

**Dimensioni Sonore** Volume 6
Bruno Nicolai
Spooky jazz and effects. Rare SP Series sleeve. (BH)

**Batterie**
Francois Auger
Drum patterns and cues. RCA Media Series sleeve. (JD)

HISTORY: Record giant moves into synchronisation throughout the late-1960s, 1970s and 1980s. OUTPUT: Frequent but hard to trace themed sets and issues. Includes film scores reissued as library cues. Introduced the (colour coded) European RCA Media Series in the late-1970s. Italian SP Series issues are rare. STYLE: Filmic, psychedelic, dramatic, electronic, experimental. MUSICIANS OF NOTE: All major Italian film composers – Ennio Morricone, Bruno Nicolai etc. SLEEVES: Early Italian issues have generic RCA top banners.

**Musiche Leggere E Gaie** Volume 2
Morricone and Poitevin
Easy and jazz cues. Classic SP Series. (JS)

# RECORD TV DISCOGRAFICA
## (RTV)

**Armature Tonali**
Franco Goldani
Drama and suspense cues. (JH)

HISTORY: Small Rome based label. OUTPUT: Minimal with very small distribution, possibly less than thirty LPs issued. Hard to find, desirable recordings. STYLE: Electronics, jazz, conceptual. MUSICIANS OF NOTE: Sandro Brugnolini, Franco Goldani. SLEEVES: Generic graphic style with colour changes in grey, yellow and pink.

## REGENCY LINE

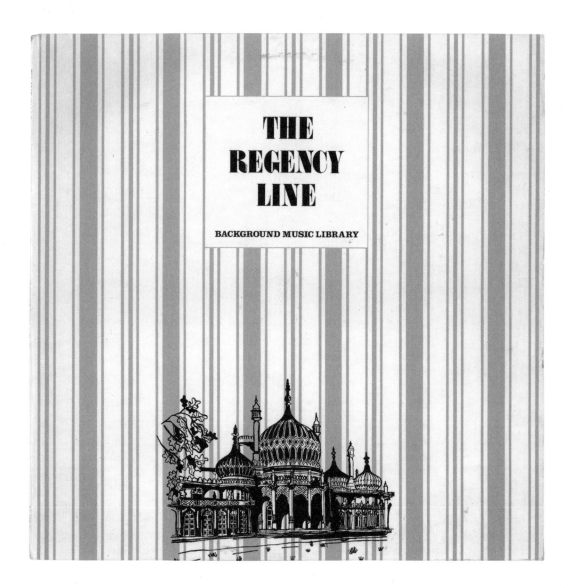

**The Regency Line**
Various moods and artists
A rare early sampler.(JG)

HISTORY: Small label from the UK, based in Brighton, c.1970. OUTPUT: Small but impressive, thirty LPs issued. Poor distribution. Now rare. STYLE: Jazz, pop, rock, dramatics, some electronics. MUSICIANS OF NOTE: Chris Rae. SLEEVES: Generic striped bag with an illustration of the Brighton pavilion. Simple colour changes.

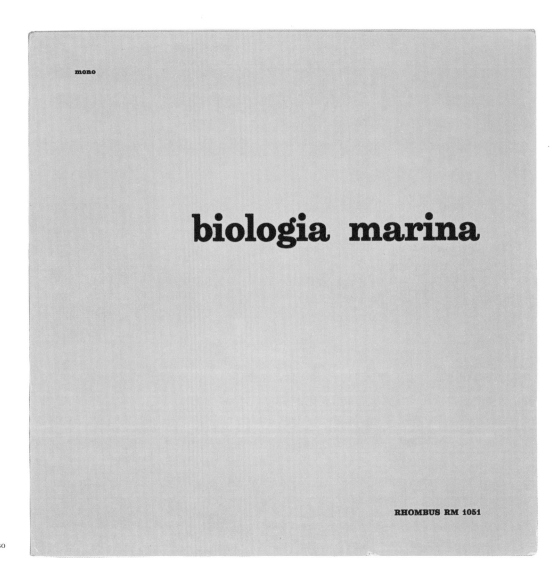

mono

# biologia marina

RHOMBUS RM 1051

**Biologia Marina**
Includes Alessandroni, Giovanni Tomasso
Underwater experimental cues. (JD)

HISTORY: Italian label, started late-1970s. OUTPUT: Small. Catalogue numbers suggest over fifty, but rarely seen recordings. Italian only distribution. STYLE: Progressive, minimal, avant-garde, experimental. MUSICIANS OF NOTE: Alessandro Alessandroni. SLEEVES: Two colour only. High quality vinyl and thick card sleeves.

## ROBERT E. VIGIER
### (REV)

# the pink magic

**The Pink Magic**
George Arvanitas Trio
Slow and medium tempo jazz styles. (S)

HISTORY: Mid to late-1970s label, French origin. Small offshoot of Sonimage.   OUTPUT: Short runs, possibly only ten issues. Sparse, very basic information about releases.
STYLE: Euro jazz, mainly composed by Vigier himself.   SLEEVES: One-colour designs using illustration.

# ROTARY

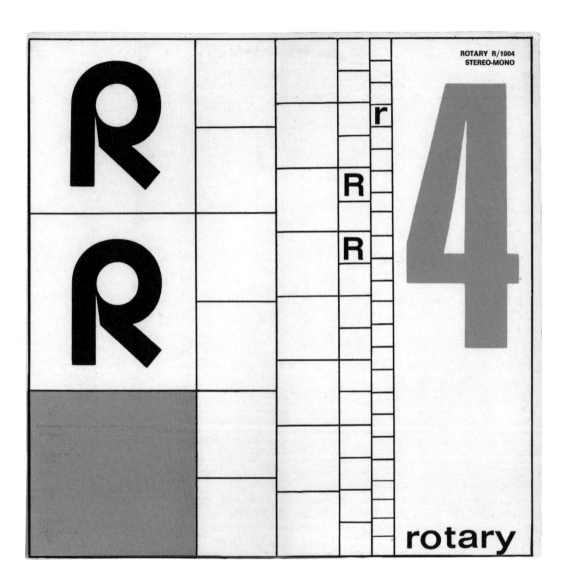

ROTARY R/1004
STEREO-MONO

rotary

**Jazz Video** Rotary 4
Farlocco (aka Guiliano Sorgini)
Dark jazz moods. (JT)

HISTORY: **Cult Italian based independent label, active around 1974.** OUTPUT: **Very small, possibly less than ten issues, only four traced to date.** STYLE: **Jazzy, moody, experimental.** SLEEVES: **Generic grid design with simple colour and number changes.**

# ROUGE

**Superdoop**
Simon Park
Electronic music by Chameleon. (MG)

**Cobra**
H. Haseley and E. Marving
Wide variety of melodic group numbers. (JM)

HISTORY: Founded in 1973, a subsidiary of the giant De Wolfe library. OUTPUT: Medium size. STYLE: Rock to electronics and beyond. SLEEVES: Graphics and illustration. Distinctive De Wolfe style.

**Glass Head**
F. McDonald and C. Rae
Very modern group sounds, funky rock. (LV)

**Hard As Rock**
J. Bunny-Browne
Guitar based rock played by Knockout. (MG)

**Blackout**
A. Valotti
Dramatic group pieces. Sleeve design by Logo Ltd. (JM)

**Red Kite**
Astral Sounds
Electronic music for water and nature. (JD)

## RYTHM AND BLUES

Georgio and The Heaven Blues
Light jazz. (JG)

The Heaven Blues
More light jazz. (JG)

HISTORY: Mid-1960s Paris based label.  OUTPUT: Small number of pressings, only a handful of releases. Produced and distributed via SIMM. Now rare.  STYLE: Fairly straight mood themes, some jazz.  SLEEVES: Graphics and paintings. No LP titles, instead they are all named after the groups who recorded the music.

# SABLE

**Andros**
Mixer
Odd futuristic sounds. (JD)

HISTORY: An obscure Italian label, late-1970s.  OUTPUT: Very small, hard to trace.  STYLE: Fairly standard library cues, also some contemporary electronics.  MUSICIANS OF NOTE: Pseudonyms mostly used.  SLEEVES: Bizarre collage.

**117 Futurissimo**
Egisto Macchi
Experimental electronic Italian sounds. (JD)

HISTORY: A continuation of the Paris based Montparnasse 2000 label. OUTPUT: Medium sized and consistent, using international artists and licensing – mostly from Italian labels such as Sermi and Gemelli. STYLE: All styles, from easy to experimental, some fine percussion. MUSICIANS OF NOTE: Piero Umiliani, Alessandro Alessandroni. SLEEVES: Strong graphic style. Some illustration.

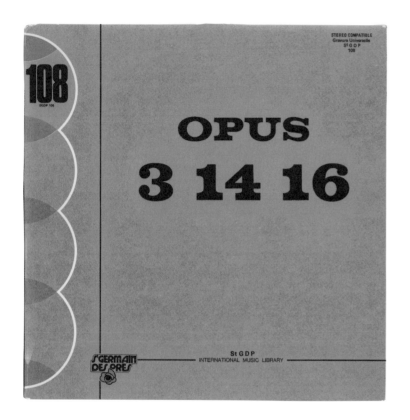

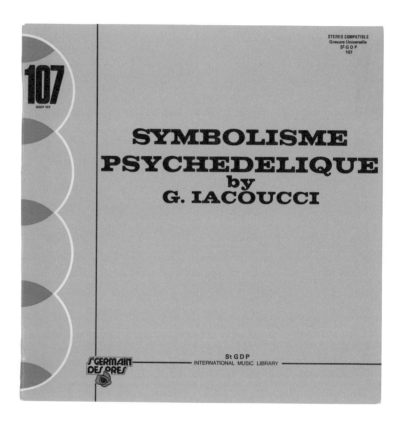

108 **OPUS 3 14 16**
A. Et L. Saint
Progressive sounds. (JG)

107 **Symbolisme Psychedelique**
G. Iacoucci
Weird atmospheres, space. (JH)

Stereo 9111 (🄫) 2292

selected sound

MONTAGE
MUSIC by GERHARD TREDE

9111

**Montage**
Gerhard Trede
German musical experiments. (JD)

HISTORY: Large German label of quality. OUTPUT: Expansive standard and experimental catalogue with very broad international distribution. Now owned by EMI. STYLE: Proggy, rocky and percussive, conceptual library recordings, some jazz and easy. MUSICIANS OF NOTE: Roland Kovac, Klaus Weiss. SLEEVES: Large family of distinctive gold sleeves.

# SERMI (SR)

SP Series
Armando Trovajoli and I Marc 4
Italian mood music
meets swinging London. (JT)

HISTORY: Italian label founded in 1967, started by Alessandro Alessandroni for experimental and library purposes. Part of the Sermi film group. OUTPUT: Prolific but obscure releases, mainly Italian only distribution. Random sub-licensing to the UK (Conroy) and France (St Germain Des Prés). Some vanity pressings. Now rare. STYLE: Broad and varied, classical, baroque, experimental, jazz and psychedelia. MUSICIANS OF NOTE: Alessandro Alessandroni, Armando Trovajoli, I Marc 4, Giovanne Tommaso. SLEEVES: Varied, including graphics, photographs and drawings. No definitive house style. Pressing inconsistencies.

**Indefinitive Atmosphere** SP Series
Giovanne Tommaso
Bass driven jazz and avant jazz. (JT)

**Open Air Parade** ST Series
Alessandro Alessandroni
Psychedelic jazz and psychedelic easy. (JT)

**Rebus** ST Series
Alessandro Alessandroni
Experimental oddities and atmospheres. (JT)

**Intermezzi** No. 4. SR Jazz Series
Alessandro Alessandroni
Folded sleeve.
Includes *Yazz In Calcutta* (sic). (JT)

# SOLEIL MASQUE

SMA 33 002

**Black Sun**
Various artists
Tangos and oriental themes.
Photograph by Yves Van Waerbeke. (S)

HISTORY: **Obscure Paris based label, c.1972.** OUTPUT: **Very few releases, less than five traced.** STYLE: **Mixture of jazz and easy-based classical.** SLEEVES: **An unpredictable blend of images and type.**

SMA 33001

THE BOSS MUSIC

Volume 1          Kitten Kind

**The Boss Music** Volume 1. Kitten Kind
Jean Claude Pierric
Jazz. (S)

# SONIMAGE

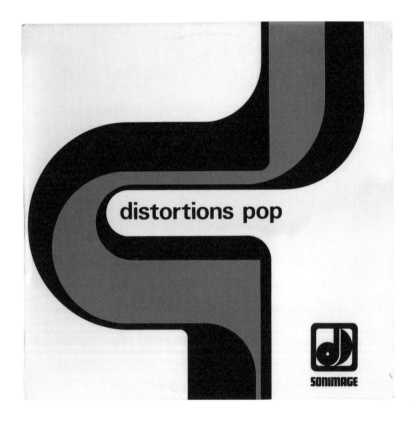

**Distortions Pop**
H. Tical
Experimental rhythmic music. Classic twisted road design. (S)

**Escalade**
Teddy Lasry
Includes *Africa*. (S)

HISTORY: Classic French label based in Boulogne, mid-1970s to mid-1980s. OUTPUT: Prolific, some original sessions and some sub-licensed recordings from Italy. STYLE: Wide ranging catalogue, from experimental pop with electronics to free jazz sessions. MUSICIANS OF NOTE: Teddy Lasry, Guiliano Sorgini. SLEEVES: Generic house sleeve with twisted road design. Later used photography and illustration.

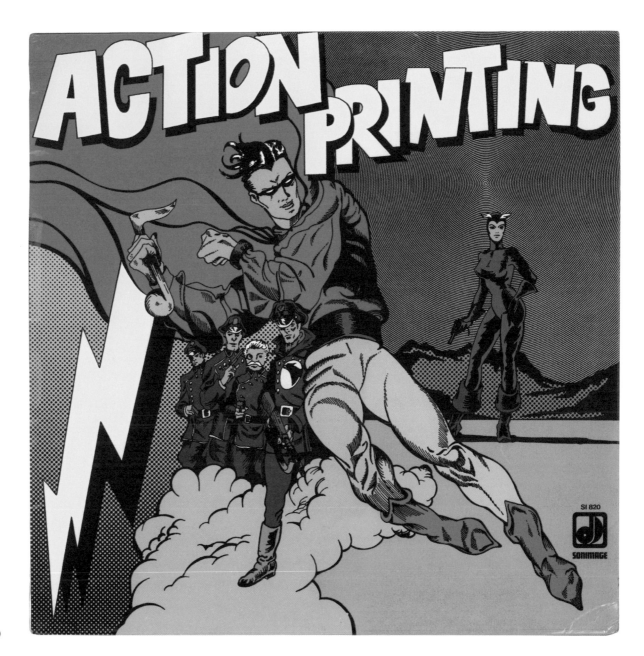

**Action Printing**
Teddy Lasry
Contemporary synthesizer sounds. (JD)

**London Transport**
Guiliano Sorgini
Beat group numbers with a psychedelic feel. (JT)

**Love Valley**
Teddy Lasry and L. Sinorcini
Romantic, nostalgic and tragic themes. (JD)

**Town**
Jean Michel Hervé
Beat synthesizer sounds. (JD)

# SONOTON

SON105 **Contemporary Sounds and Movements** Volume 2
Maladen Franko
New sounds for current affairs. (JM)

SON168 **The Micro Chip Revolution**
Sam Sklair and Gus Galbraith
Electronics. (JM)

HISTORY: The largest independent German library, based in Munich, founded by Gerard Narholz in the 1960s. OUTPUT: Huge, worldwide and diverse. Music also licensed internationally. STYLE: All musical fields covered, notably jazz, electronics, easy and disco. MUSICIANS OF NOTE: John Fiddy. SLEEVES: Photography effects, stock images.

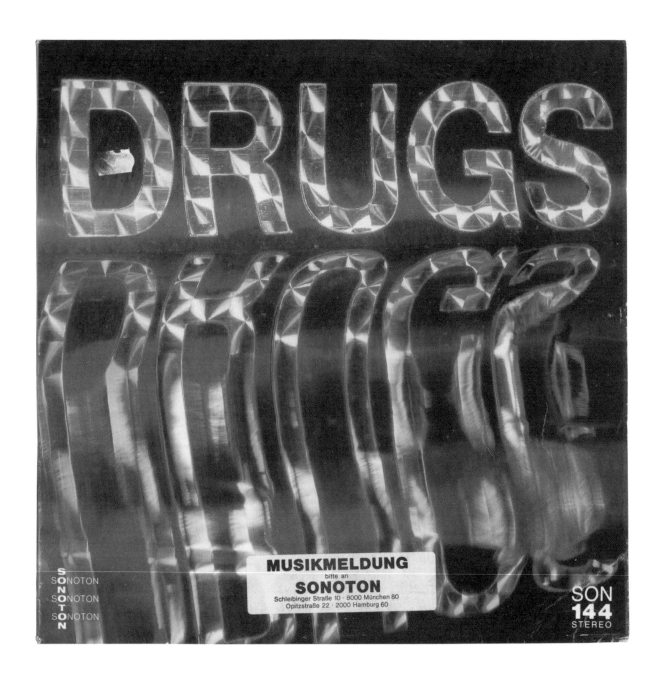

SON144 **Drugs**
Sven Torstenson
Modern psychedelics. (JD)

SON130 **Slow**
John Fiddy and Sammy Burdson
Contemporary light sounds. (SS)

SON131 **Fast**
Francis Monkman and John Fiddy
Contemporary heavy sounds. (SS)

SON101 **Amazing Space** Volume 1
Mladen Franko
Experimental themes. (JD)

SON113 **Under Water** Volume 1
Walt Rockman (JD)

SON178 **Sport Sequences** Volume 2
Klaus Weiss
Light / heavy activity. (JD)

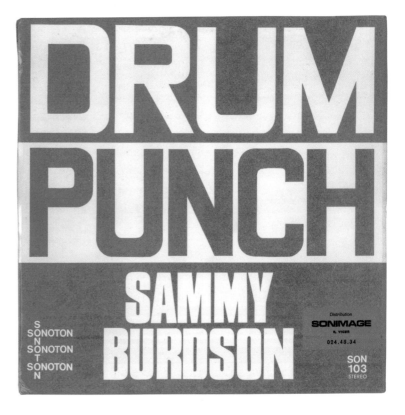

SON122 **Swinging Centuries** Volume 1
Various artists
Updated period music. (JD)

SON103 **Drum Punch**
Sammy Burdson
Percussive cues. (JD)

## SOUNDS OF BROADCASTING

Standard SOB sleeve.
No artists' credits. (LV)

HISTORY: **Part of the William B. Tanner Company. Memphis based, possibly mid-1970s.** OUTPUT: **Large and varied.** STYLE: **Vast range of classical and electronic background styles.** MUSICIANS OF NOTE: **No musicians ever credited.** SLEEVES: **Generic golden house style.**

## SOUND WORKSHOP

**Olimpiade** SWS111
Satucci Scoppa
Rare sporting themes, jazz instrumentation.
MP2000 distribution sticker. (JG)

HISTORY: Independent Italian label, started by composer and artist Piero Umiliani in the late-1960s. Linked with the Liuto label, many pressings credit both labels. OUTPUT: Original jazz sessions, rare soundtrack scores also pressed for background usage. Very poor international distribution. Highly sought after recordings. STYLE: Varied in style and quality, some improvisation and electronics mixed with folk. MUSICIANS OF NOTE: Alessandro Alessandroni and Piero Umiliani himself. Pseudonyms also used. SLEEVES: House style on the reverse only. Collage and graphics dominate. Inconsistent catalogue numbers.

**La Ragazza Fuoristrada**
Piero Umiliani
Full score as background music. (S)

**Due Temi Con Variazioni** c.1977
Rovi
Jazz improvisations. (I)

**L'Uomo e la Citta**
Piero Umiliani
Also a Liuto release. (S)

**News!!! News!!!**
Moggi (Piero Umiliani)
Jazz and documentary style cues. (I)

**The Folk Group**
Zalla
Rock sounds, includes *Underworld.* (JT)

# SOUTHERN

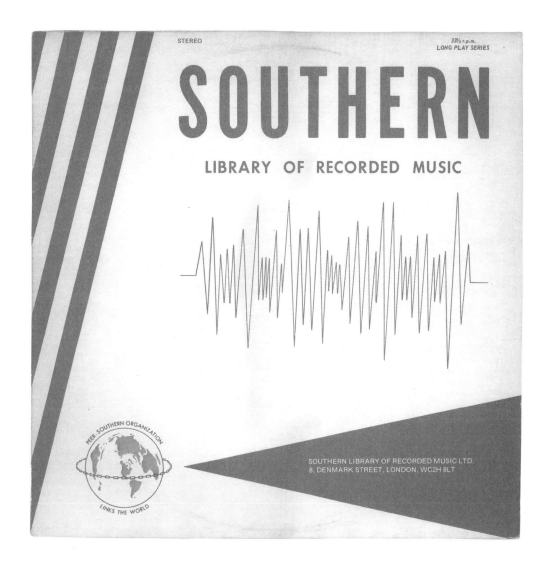

Standard Southern UK sleeve. (JT)

HISTORY: London label based in Denmark Street, mid-1960s onwards. Run by Dennis Berry (aka Peter Dennis) who also started the contemporary mood music label known as Peer International. Many LPs from Peer repressed as Southern recordings. OUTPUT: Catalogue of about fifty pressings. Large international distribution network. Licensed recordings from international artists, no original sessions. Some rare 7" issues, with non-LP tracks. STYLE: European easy, jazz, classical, percussion and electronics. MUSICIANS OF NOTE: Nino Nardini, Johnny Scott, Bernard Ebbinghouse. SLEEVES: Generic sleeves in blue and white house style.

# SQUIRREL

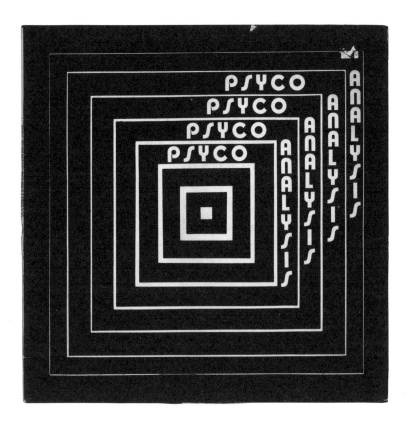

**Psyco Analysis**
Corviria
Electronics and pastoral sounds. (JT)

**Accadde A.......**
Arawak
Experimental cues. (SS)

HISTORY: Small independent Italian label, c.1972.  OUTPUT: Restricted distribution, small output of possibly fifteen releases.  STYLE: Experimental, dramatic.  MUSICIANS OF NOTE: All artists used pseudonyms.  SLEEVES: Mixture of styles using graphics and painting.

# STANDARD

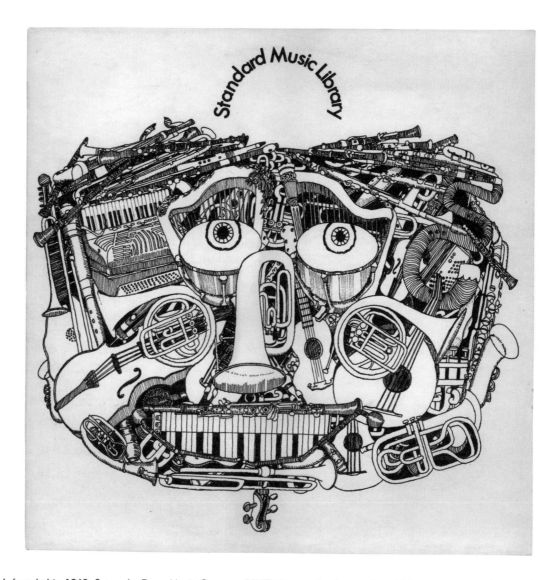

Standard Music Library

Early single colour 'face' sleeve. (JT)

HISTORY: **Vast independent London label, founded in 1968. Set up by Essex Music Group and LWT, this was the first music publishing company to be owned jointly with a broadcaster.** OUTPUT: **Large and regular pressings throughout the 1960s and 1970s.** STYLE: **All styles produced, from big band to electronic experimentation.** MUSICIANS OF NOTE: **Brian Eno, David Vorhaus, Herbie Flowers, Delia Derbyshire, Ron Grainer, Sam Fonteyn.** SLEEVES: **Single colour face made-up of musical instruments, changing to film strip colour sleeve in the late-1970s. Earlier sleeves are laminated.** FAMOUS CUES: *Catweasel, On The Buses, Please Sir, Budgie, Crimestoppers.*

studio **G**

LPSG 4002 Volume 4

**Images**

**Images**
P. Willsher and T. Kelly
Disco, and modern rhythms. (JM)

HISTORY: Medium sized but far reaching British label, established in early 1970 by John Gale, hence the 'G' in Studio G.  OUTPUT: Averaged sized with some rare and experimental 7" vinyl.  STYLE: Rock, jazz, horror, humour, electronics.  SLEEVES: Period graphics, normally two colour process printing. All sleeves have theme logos in the bottom right corner.  FAMOUS CUES: *The Chesty Morgan* theme, *Drag Racing* used for BBC Snooker, *Vision-On* incidentals.

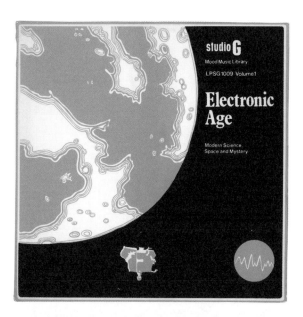

**Dramatic and Horror**
Paul Lewis, David De Lara, Robert Cornford, James Harpham, Stan Medcalf
Tension, suspense, shock. (JM)

**Descriptive Suites**
Paul Lewis and James Harpham (SS)

**Electronic Age**
Electronics, concrete, voodoo.
Artwork by Nina Klein. (SS)

**Drama and Horror**
Paul Lewis
Dark movements in jazz. (JT)

**Cool Beat**
Robert Cornford
Heavy dance numbers. (JG)

**Avant Garde**
D. Detoni, John Keliehor, John Lewis
Abstract electronics and ethereal processed vocals. (C)

studio **G**

Mood Music Library

LPSG 1001 Volume 1

# Beat Group

Side A
Instrumental
Beat Group

Side B
Vocal Beat Group

**Beat Group**
Mike Lease (arranger and organist)
Progressive cues. (S)

**Racing Tempo**
Eric Towren
Fast, swinging jazz themes. 10" release. (S)

**Voices in the wind**
The Paris Studio Group
Jazz and scat themes. 10" release. (MG)

HISTORY: London based, originally songsheet publishers, part of the De Wolfe empire. Moved into 33rpm library records in the mid-1960s. OUTPUT: Medium size catalogue, high quality releases. Some sub-publishing with Musique Pour l'Image. SLEEVES: Early stunning graphics, later generic white and gold circle design.

**City In Terror / Sextopraxis**
W. Warren
Rare concept LP. Front and back cover. (S)

**Zenith**
Eric Towren
Space and underwater sounds, percussion based. (JT)

# TELEMUSIC

**Vibrations**
Bernard Lubat
Jazz beats. Standard Telemusic house sleeve in silver and grey. (JT)

**Spatial & Co**
Sauveur Mallia
Late European 'disco' sound. (JM)

HISTORY: Important Paris based organisation founded in 1968. OUTPUT: Massive international output. Some sub-licensing. Consistently high quality recordings. STYLE: Electronics, percussion, experimentals, jazz and funky rhythms. MUSICIANS OF NOTE: Bernard Lubat, Guy Pedersen, Bernard Estardy, Raymond Guiot. SLEEVES: Standard house style, with simple colour and logo variations. Later used graphics and stock photography.

# THEMES

Mystery Movie

New Blood

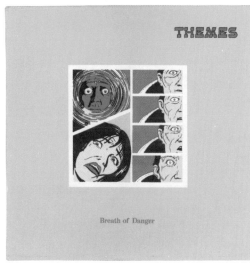

Breath of Danger

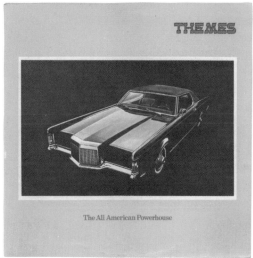

The All American Powerhouse

**Mystery Movie**
James Clarke
Driving and funky underscores. (S)

**Breath of Danger**
Hawkshaw and Bennett
Suspense and drama backcloths. (JM)

**New Blood**
Alan Parker and Alan Hawkshaw
Heavy rhythmic pop. (S)

**The All American Powerhouse**
Alan Parker and Alan Hawkshaw
Guitar based funk. (S)

HISTORY: London based library label, founded by musician Alan Parker in the mid-1970s. OUTPUT: Large catalogue developed throughout the late-1970s. Now owned by EMI. Most sessions recorded in Germany. STYLE: Rock, funk, comedy, romance. MUSICIANS OF NOTE: Alan Parker, Alan Hawkshaw. SLEEVES: Mustard colour background with illustrations in various styles. FAMOUS CUES: Drama Suites 1 & 2 used in *The Hanged Man* produced by Yorkshire TV, *Grange Hill* theme.

# TIMING

**Cradle of time** Timing No. 14
Pierre Avary
Issued as De Wolfe In Editions. (JG)

**Timing** No. 1
Stephan Grappelli and Jacky Giordano
Insane beats. (JG)

HISTORY: **Label started as part of In Editions, Paris, early-1970s.** OUTPUT: **Small, now rare. Some sub-licensing to the UK via De Wolfe.** STYLE: **Trad jazz to electronics.**
MUSICIANS OF NOTE: **Jacky Giordano, Stephan Grappelli, Pierre Avary.** SLEEVES: **Simple graphic sleeves with colour changes.**

# TITIAN

**Descriptive**
Corviria
Synthesized themes. Includes *Evil's Suite*. (JD)

HISTORY: Late-1970s Italian independent label, Milan based. OUTPUT: Small catalogue, now rare. STYLE: Filmic, quite odd. SLEEVES: Simple, graphic.

# TVMUSIC

Crazy Sounds / Weird Sounds
Cecil Leuter
Electronics. TVM house bag. (SS)

HISTORY: Part of the giant Chappell library, possibly a budget label, c.1973.   OUTPUT: Few LPs traced, possibly less than ten releases.   STYLE: Experimental, electronics, percussion.   MUSICIANS OF NOTE: Cecil Leuter.   SLEEVES: Standard blue and white disco house bag.

## UBM RECORDS
### (UWE BUSCHKÖTTER MUSIC)

**Computer Energy** UBM Volume 8
Various artists
Guitars, arp, moog, prophet work. (LV)

HISTORY: Cologne based label. Founded early-1980 by Uwe Buschkötter, a longstanding arranger of jazz and easy music. OUTPUT: Small. STYLE: Capitalising on fashionable electronic and synthesizer music of the time. SLEEVES: Simple, using a black and white graphic house style.

**Imaginations**
André Huet
Music for dance expression. (JH)

**Imaginations** / 2
André Huet
Music for dance expression. (JII)

HISTORY: Paris based label specialising in ballet and avant-garde dance music. Later moving briefly into the library and corporate music arena. OUTPUT: Few library releases, some on 7". STYLE: Experimental, industrial. MUSICIANS OF NOTE: André Huet, Sylvio Gualda. SLEEVES: Strong graphic and fantasy feel. Some photography on earlier issues.

**Metamorphoses**
F. Semprun and M. Christodoulides
More music for dance expression. (JH)

# VEDETTE

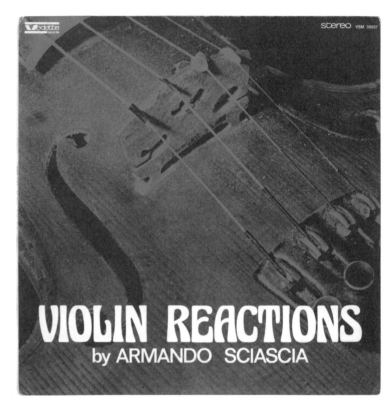

**Musica Per Tutte Le Ore** Volume 31
Features Bruno Battisti
Standard Vedette Sonorisation sleeve. (S)

**Violin Reactions**
Armando Sciascia
Electronic violin with beats. (JT)

HISTORY: Milan based label from the late-1960s onwards, started by film composer Armando Sciascia. OUTPUT: A soundtrack specialist label, but issued original scores for library usage. STYLE: Notable spaghetti style output, jazz. Also classic Italian style 'Giallo' horror themes. MUSICIANS OF NOTE: Bruno Battisti, Lesiman, Armando Sciascia. (Lesiman was a pseudonym for Paolo Renosto). SLEEVES: Standard design using three swirls, later employing photography and graphics for the different series.

**High Tension** Volume 1
Lesiman
Modern, dark dramatics and underscores. (JT)

**Here and Now 1**
Lesiman
Intense rhythmic grooves, heavy on effects. (C)

**Here and Now 2**
Lesiman
A continuation of Here and Now 1. (SS)

**Love**
Mario Molino and his Group
Rare double library LP. (S)

HISTORY: Late-1960s Italian label. OUTPUT: Small and diverse. Some licensing to Sonimage in France. Fairly poor distribution. One of the few libraries to issue double LPs. Now rare. STYLE: Alternative, rocky, a little jazz. MUSICIANS OF NOTE: Mario Molino. SLEEVES: No house style. Paintings, graphics, photography.

**La Palla é Rotonda**
Remigio Ducros
Jazz and sporting themed concepts. (JG)

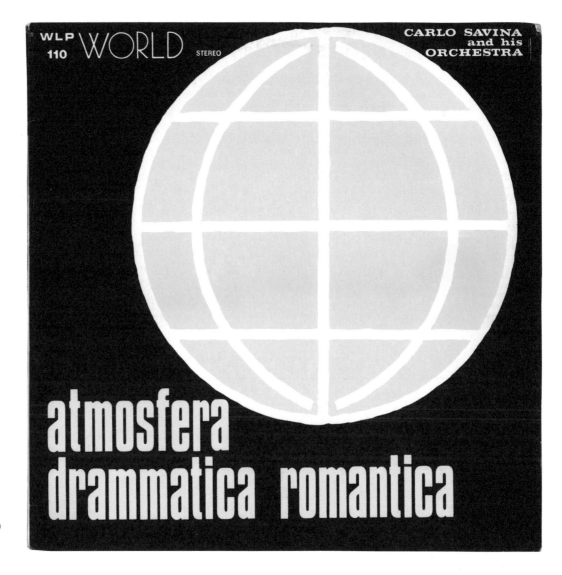

**Atmosfera Drammatica Romantica** WLP 110
Carlo Savina
Heavy drama and love. (JD)

HISTORY: Rome based organisation dating from the late-1960s. OUTPUT: Very small. Few issues, hard to trace. STYLE: Various standard dramatics and moods. MUSICIANS OF NOTE: Carlo Savina. SLEEVES: Two colour globe house style sleeves, some colour variations.

## Afterword

I think it was Mr Fraser Moss who first turned me on to library records, back when he was introducing me to all manner of arcane syncopated electronics. I soon became lost in a world of abstract percussion by delirious Frenchmen and strange mellifluous soundtracks, scored and played for non-existent adverts in Wardour Street studios.

To me it feels like a bizarre parallel world, a reflection of the styles and tropes of five hundred years of popular music. Or like a journey through the mirror, in a sequence from a seventies Hammer film, to a place where nobody knows how to distinguish between the genres: rock, jazz, pop, avant-garde, electronic, baroque, folk...

A sidereal arena to the contemporary world of pop chart positionings.

They're like concept albums. The concept is an abstract idea that's already in place and the musicians – various jazznik session musos and visionaries with effects boxes – have to interpret it. Industry in motion, landscape, contemporary baroque, anguish and mystery. I like the themes and the track descriptions – neutral underscore; nervous energy; uneasy, sparse, thick chords, disturbed – as above with spiky interjections.

The name Library has a resonance of archives, dusty volumes, musty rooms containing filed memories and ideas. And searching for these records you sometimes feel like a character in an H.P. Lovecraft story, discovering arcane tomes in dusty backrooms and Parisian flea markets. For me its always been about the strange atmospheres etched into the vinyl – not breakbeats or the more obvious DJ sample fodder.

And perfectly reflecting all of this are the sleeves. Beguiling abstractions and collages, wonky typography, a bad but good design free for all, unfettered by commercial constraints (well, they're for commercial use but not in the record shop / chart market place). There are great series of sleeves, simple pop art geometry and colour coding that demands that you hunt down every one. The truly bizarre collages on some, bordering on outsider art, fit perfectly with the angular, disjointed moods of the music – as if the musicians and designer are working from the same brief.

The sleeves have been a huge influence on me, for their brash pop surrealism (rivaled only by Polish film posters), their subtle but clunky type and their simple multiple sleeves with colour changes.

Working with bands like Stereolab and Broadcast inspires a way of designing which represents the album, its colours, tone and vision. Packaging that's wrapped inside the music.

**Julian House**

Jonny Trunk started Trunk Records in 1995. The first release was the library compilation 'The Super Sounds Of Bosworth'. Still obsessed by library and film music, Trunk continues to issue rare lost recordings, DJs internationally, broadcasts through the medium of television and radio and sources beautiful and often strange music for television and film.

**This book has been a dream for many years, and has only been made possible thanks to Fuel and the record collections of the fellow library fanatics I've met over the last decade. JT**

## THE CONTRIBUTORS

**Cherrystones (C)**  Recording artist, compiler and remarkably dark DJ.
**Jerry Dammers (JD)**  Former 'Special'.
**Jazzman Gerald (JG)**  Deals in soulfunkjazzlatinlibrarysoundtracks.
**Martin Green (MG)**  DJ to the stars.
**Ben Horner (BH)**  Artist and painter.
**Julian House (JH)**  Graphic designer at Intro.
**Intoxica! (I)**  Legendary vintage record store on Portobello Road, London.
**Joel Martin (JM)**  Early library entrepreneur, DJ and collector.
**Fraser Moss (FM)**  Head designer at You Must Create.
**Sermad (S)**  Obsessive library fiend.
**Justin Spear (JS)**  DJ, collector, writer and occasional broadcaster.
**Steve Stasis (SS)**  Beat maker, collector and sound engineer.
**Jonny Trunk (JT)**
**John Tye (LO)**  Head of Lo Recordings.
**Luke Vibert (LV)**  International DJ, artist and collector.
**Patrick Whitaker (PW)**  aka 'The Quadfather', film fashion designer.

Further thanks must go to the following: Warren De Wolfe and Steve Rosie at De Wolfe Music, George Barker at JW Media Music, Cliff Simms at Standard Library, Howard Friend at Bosworths, Juliette Richards at BMG Zomba, Pascal Armand, Godsey for research on all his (C) LPs, Richard Dawson at Happy Retouching, Honey Luard.

NOTE: This book catalogues music of the 1960s and 1970s. Some of the record labels are still in existence today and it must be understood that our musical style information does not take into consideration contemporary recordings.

'Output' refers to the number of titles the library issued. Where possible exact LP issue numbers are used, otherwise estimates have been given.

This is by no means a definitive guide to libraries. The following labels have been traced but we were unable to feature them in this book: Ariston, Ayna, Black Rock, CEM, Duse, Dingles, Fly, Fono Film, Horse Shoe, Jammy, KTS, Novoton, Pegaso, Picci, Red Bus, RKM, Studio One.

Every effort has been made to contact the libraries to obtain permission for the reproduction of the sleeves in this publication. We apologise to those we were unable to contact.

Useful links:

www.trunkrecords.com
www.jazzmanrecords.co.uk
www.intoxica.co.uk
www.thesoundlibrary.com
www.moviegrooves.com
www.vinylvulture.co.uk
www.b-music.co.uk
www.lorecordings.com
www.hub100.com
www.recordlibrarymusic.co.uk

Recommended further listening:

Abstractions Of The Industrial North, Basil Kirchin (Trunk Records)
Unreleased Music from Romero's Dawn Of The Dead, Various (Trunk Records)
Bite Hard, The Music De Wolfe Studio Sampler, Various (BBE Records)
Le Jazz Beat Volumes 1 & 2, Various (Jazzman Records)
Luke Vibert presents Nuggets, Various (Lo Recordings)
Luke Vibert presents Further Nuggets, Various (Lo Recordings)
Barry 7 Connectors Volumes 1 & 2, Various (Lo Recordings)
Stereo Ultra Volumes 1, 2 & 3, Various (Sirocco)
Cinemaphonic, Various (Emperor Norton)
Lift Off, Various (Apollo Sound)
Funk Cinematique, Various (Plastic)
Kaleidoscopia, Various (Plastic)
Blow Up Volume 1 & 2, Various (Blow Up Records)
Soundbook 1 & 2, Various (Douce)
Scoctopus, Various (Schema)
Soho Lounge Beat, Various (EMI)